THE ONLY
WAY OUT IS

Hay House Titles of Related Interest

YOU CAN HEAL YOUR LIFE, the movie,
starring Louise L. Hay & Friends
(available as a 1-DVD program and an expanded 2-DVD set)
Watch the trailer at: **www.LouiseHayMovie.com**

COSMIC ORDERING FOR BEGINNERS:
Everything You Need to Know to Make It Work for You,
by Barbel Mohr and Clemens Maria Mohr

ENERGY SECRETS: *The Ultimate Well-Being Plan,*
by Alla Svirinskaya

**THE GURU OF JOY: *Sri Sri Ravi Shankar
& the Art of Living,*** by François Gautier

**MAXIMIZE YOUR POTENTIAL THROUGH THE POWER
OF YOUR SUBCONSCIOUS MIND FOR HEALTH AND
VITALITY,** by Dr. Joseph Murphy

**POWER OF THE SOUL: *Inside Wisdom
for an Outside World,*** by John Holland

10 STEPS TO TAKE CHARGE OF YOUR EMOTIONAL LIFE:
*Overcoming Anxiety, Distress, and Depression Through
Whole-Person Healing,* by Eve A. Wood, M.D.

All of the above are available at your
local bookstore, or may be ordered by visiting

Hay House USA: **www.hayhouse.com**®
Hay House Australia: **www.hayhouse.com.au**
Hay House UK: **www.hayhouse.co.uk**
Hay House South Africa: **www.hayhouse.co.za**
Hay House India: **www.hayhouse.co.in**

THE ONLY WAY OUT IS

Within

Clear Your Energy System
and Keep Yourself Emotionally
and Physically Healthy

Rohini Singh

HAY
HOUSE

HAY HOUSE, INC.
Carlsbad, California • New York City
London • Sydney • Johannesburg
Vancouver • Hong Kong • New Delhi

Copyright © 2008 by Rohini Singh

Published and distributed in the United States by: Hay House, Inc.: www.
hayhouse.com • *Published and distributed in Australia by:* Hay House
Australia Pty. Ltd.: www.hayhouse.com.au • *Published and distributed
in the United Kingdom by:* Hay House UK, Ltd.: www.hayhouse.co.uk •
Published and distributed in the Republic of South Africa by: Hay House
SA (Pty), Ltd.: www.hayhouse.co.za • *Distributed in Canada by:* Raincoast:
www.raincoast.com • *Published in India by:* Hay House Publishers India:
www.hayhouse.co.in

Editorial supervision: Jill Kramer • *Design:* Tricia Breidenthal

The author of this book does not dispense medical advice or prescribe
the use of any technique as a form of treatment for physical, emotional,
or medical problems without the advice of a physician, either directly or
indirectly. The intent of the author is only to offer information of a general
nature to help you in your quest for emotional and spiritual well-being. In
the event you use any of the information in this book for yourself, which is
your constitutional right, the author and the publisher assume no responsibility for your actions.

Library of Congress Cataloging-in-Publication Data

Singh, Rohini.
    The only way out is within : clear your energy system and keep yourself
emotionally and physically healthy / Rohini Singh.
        p. cm.
    ISBN-13: 978-1-4019-2011-1 (tradepaper) 1. Success--Psychological
aspects. 2. Well-being. 3. Self-actualization (Psychology) 4. Control
(Psychology) I. Title.
    BF637.S8S5457 2008
    158.1

ISBN: 978-1-4019-2011-1

11 10 09 08   4 3 2 1
1st edition, October 2008

Printed in the United States of America

Contents

Preface

The ideas in this book aren't new. It would be presumptuous on my part to claim that they're original. All I can say is that the understanding and expression of them are my own. I've written about what I've experienced, internalized, and come to deeply believe in.

While I was working on this book, I read a paragraph from Rainer Maria Rilke's *Letters to a Young Poet* in which he advises an aspiring poet to "write about what your everyday life offers you: describe your sorrows and desires; the thoughts that pass through your mind; and your belief in some kind of beauty—describe all these with heartfelt, humble sincerity and, when you express yourself, use the Things around you, the images from your dreams, and the objects that you remember."

This I have tried to do. My everyday life provided the content, the characters, and the story. My experiences—joys and sorrows, success and failure, hopes and desires—were the teachers who tutored me patiently, day after day, until I'd learned what they had to teach. In all the examples that give the book life, I'm sure you'll see glimpses of the things around me, the images from my dreams, and the objects that I remember. Heartfelt, humble sincerity is what I hope will come through on every page.

Read this book with your heart, not just your mind. If it touches a chord, I pray that it serves to propel you on your own unique journey of growth.

— **R.S.**

※ ※ ※

Chapter 1

GETTING UP ON THE RIGHT SIDE OF YOUR BED!

"We are born into the world of nature;
our second birth is the world of the spirit."

— BHAGAVAD GITA

Seeker, reader, book browser, or *window-shopper:* How shall I address you? You, who have bought this book, or are considering doing so. If you can't make up your mind, let me ask you one clarifying question: *Why would you add one more volume to your already considerable collection?* You may love buying these self-help books with attractive titles that not only promise peace of mind, happiness, growth, and self-awareness but also offer mantras on how to become healthy, wealthy, and wise. The majority ultimately say the same thing, don't they? One of them should be enough. Often, I suppose, you get tempted by titles. Maybe this one attracted you; it would, because most of us are seeking physical and emotional well-being.

So let me ask you again: *Who are you—a seeker, reader, browser, or window-shopper?* And this time, I'm posing my question a little more seriously.

If you're a window-shopper, you've set out with no definite sense of purpose. You'll wander around aimlessly, allowing appealing mannequins to seduce you into entering shops to buy things you don't need. You'll have a cup of coffee along the way, and when it's time to return, you'll go back home, carrying purchases you'll forget about as soon as they've found a place in your closet. Please don't buy this book. You will do the same to it.

I'm sorry, browser—you don't need this book, either. Make a note of the title if it intrigues you, but no, don't buy it until you've read the stack that lies unopened at home. Of course you *mean* to read them all, but obviously it's not yet such a burning priority. Forget this one.

Reader, I can't fault you for not absorbing all that *you've* bought. You have a voracious appetite for the written word, and you will have finished this small book before the day is over. You'll judge it, label it, and put it back on your bookshelf or pass it on to the next friend who shows some interest in it. Well, I can tell you, you might enjoy the contents . . . but are you willing to put in the effort for emotional and physical wellness? I don't know. Reconsider before you spend your hard-earned money.

Seeker, this book is for you. No, not because it's saying anything very new, but because new words aren't what you're looking for. You're searching for something more profound. Anything and everything around you is a trigger for your own insights, a deeper exploration of yourself. This book will also help in this process. In fact, what it's saying has very little to do with the decision as to whether or not you should buy it. The real decision has to do with what you plan to *do* with the book, which is directly connected to what priority you've given to yourself and your growth.

What do these words mean? If you're a window-shopper in your life, they mean very little. You haven't set your course yet. Browser, you occasionally flirt with the idea of making yourself priority number one, but it's a mere flirtation, a novel idea. It hasn't yet turned into the passionate quest that can keep you inspired. Reader, you "know" it all, but your knowledge remains between the covers of books. You haven't allowed it to touch and transform you. Seeker, you'll enjoy this work because, as I've said, mere content isn't what you're pursuing. This isn't why you buy a new book. You allow words to penetrate you, deposit the seed, and give birth to new ideas and concepts. You're open in your thinking. You're aroused. You're the highest priority in your own life.

And this is a workbook for your daily life, not comfortable bedside reading. Study the title very carefully. If you agree that the only way out is within *and* you're willing to pay the price to break free, buy this book and take it home. And let's start work right away.

Let's begin with the first thing you do every morning: getting out of bed. And let's figure out the right way to do it!

— Consider this modern-day scenario: A man is getting ready to go to work. As he woke up earlier in the morning, his first thought was of the meeting he has scheduled later in the day. It's a very important sit-down with a foreign delegation that can win him a huge contract and pitch him into international headlines. It could well be the turning point in his career that he has always prayed for. He has been working on the deal for over a year now, and today it will finally come to fruition. He dresses carefully and tells his wife that he'll be leaving early so he can reach the office in time to look into the last-minute details and fine-tune everything.

He gets into a taxi and becomes engrossed in working on his laptop. After a while, when he looks up, he realizes that the car is stuck in a massive traffic jam. Lanes of vehicles stand bumper to bumper, hopelessly stranded. At the slightest sign of movement, motorcycles, scooters, and buses single-mindedly push their way in, trying to press ahead, quite unconcerned about others. The jam tightens. The man looks nervously at his watch. If they move within the next five minutes, he will just about make it in time for the crucial meeting. With mounting despair, he realizes that this is not going to happen.

Angrily, he snaps at the driver: Why did he take *this* route today?! He closes his laptop in irritation and tosses it on the seat beside him. His agitation increases by the second. How could this have happened, and why today of all days? The question repeats itself mercilessly in his mind. Fifteen minutes later, they still haven't moved an inch. Unable to control his rage and disappointment, he calls the office on his cell phone. His secretary tells him that the foreign delegation has already arrived and is waiting for him. She requests that he come quickly, as they have other important appointments to keep. Frustration and helplessness break through as he fires off another volley of angry abuse at the hapless driver.

— Here is how another day begins: A woman wakes up, and as she stretches, a delicious sense of expectancy runs through her. Finally, this is the day her baby will come home. How long she's waited for this moment! Almost two years back, she decided that she would adopt a child. The whole process has taken this much time. But now that the day is here and she has seen and held the baby who will be "hers," it has blotted out the agony of waiting, the uncertainty, and all her apprehensions. There's only one final formality left, which she's rushing out now to complete. She believes in auspicious days, and today is the one that her astrologer has chosen for this homecoming.

She takes one final look around the room. Everything is in place. She looks fondly at the new crib, piles of diapers, and small clothes and, smiling to herself, gets into her car. She looks at her watch. She'll be right on time. Today she needs to be—the official who will witness her signing of the papers will be there for just a half hour. She turns the corner, and suddenly the good cheer vanishes: She's confronted with a line of unmoving cars ahead. Quickly, she considers whether she can change routes, but it's already too late. There are cars behind her, too, and in any case this is the only way to reach the adoption center.

She looks at her watch. There's still no cause for despair. She'll make it, although just in the nick of time. Fifteen minutes later, that hope has faded away. There has been a major accident, and she realizes that it will take hours to clear the traffic.

How could this have happened to her today? The auspicious day will pass, and it will not have turned out the way she'd planned. How can she return home without a baby in her arms? A sharp wave of disappointment floods through her. Tears flow as she gropes in her bag to find her cell phone to call the center. She feels drained, helpless, and impotent. But then as she sits there, tears still silently flowing, she realizes that there's nothing she can do about it. The situation is out of her control. She'll have to reschedule the meeting. She calms herself with this thought.

— In a different part of the city, another man wakes up at dawn. He walks out onto his balcony, greeting the day with a gentle smile. As he sips his tea, he thinks back on his career and contemplates what a special day today is, as it is the one when he'll be recognized for his singing prowess by no less than the President, who will present him with an award at a grand function. His children have come from all over the world especially for the occasion. He feels blessed and grateful.

His wife has bought him new clothes for the ceremony, and they are lovingly laid out on the bed. He begins to dress. Soon they are all on their way, a proud family. They're just ten minutes away from the venue when their car is stopped. The traffic is being diverted. The police officer who leans down into the window tells them there's an important function that the President has to attend. His cavalcade will be passing this way shortly. No traffic is to be allowed through until then.

In vain, they try to explain how important it is for *them* to reach the venue as well for the award-presentation ceremony. If they're late, they point out, they'll be denied entry. The police officer looks at them helplessly. He understands their plight, but there's nothing he can do about it.

Disappointment is palpable in the car as it becomes evident that they might not make it by the appointed time. The man himself looks unshaken, though. With the same equanimity with which he drank his morning tea, he inserts a CD into the player. He leans back and is soon absorbed in the music, oblivious to the honking cars and his family's tension.

The point of these three vignettes is obvious. All three people are poised at very significant junctures in their lives. The events are of equal importance. The traffic jams they encounter are a metaphor for the hurdles they come up against on their journeys that prevent them from reaching their destinations. That's a given, but what makes the three scenarios differ is how each individual handles the "roadblock."

If I asked you which of the responses you'd choose, you would probably say the third, while at the same time wondering if this was rather idealistic.

Why are the responses so different? And which one do *you* most identify with? Do you see yourself as reactive, easily frustrated, impatient, and quick to get angry and tense? Or would you fit more accurately into the second category—your responses are more controlled and less intense? You get upset but manage to calm yourself soon enough. Or do you relate to the third situation? This means that you remain quite unfazed by life's challenges; you certainly know how to flow with the tide, to change tracks, and to remain cool under stress.

Actually, you belong to all three categories. On certain days you resemble the angry, agitated man; on others, under the same provocation, you're quite controlled and accepting; and yes, there are also times when a very similar situation doesn't throw you at all.

What causes these swings, and are they in any way controllable? If you think the answer is no, you're in for a big surprise.

That's where getting out of bed the right way comes in! "Getting up on the wrong side" of your bed is another way of saying that on a particular day your energy is depleted. You're cranky, irritable, and prone to be reactive. Anything and everything seems to trigger a snappy retort, and often others bear the brunt of your outbursts. On other days, you're more centered, calm, and poised. No task seems too big to take on. You handle challenges with ease. You're expansive in your dealings with others. On some days, the world looks "gray" and purposeless . . . on others, "rosy" and joyful. You may be unaware that your "mood," as you think of it, actually reflects your energy system.

The energy I'm speaking of here isn't just physical energy, but a more subtle kind: the prana, chi, ki, or life force. This invisible *energy system* is your bedrock, the very basis of your well-being. The attitudes and the responses you choose at a particular moment hinge on it. The quality of your day—and from a bigger perspective, your life—depends on it. Yet it's a system most of us are woefully unaware of. Hence, we feel bewildered when on a particular day we find it hard to cope with something small, while on another, we effortlessly manage to do so much more with so little effort. With frustration, and often irritation, we feel "let down" because we're unable to sustain the good "moods." Since we aren't aware that it's the energy system that's responsible for these incomprehensible fluctuations, we can do little to keep it clean, free of clutter, and functioning at peak efficiency.

In the chapters ahead, you will come to understand how to . . .

. . . gauge the efficiency of your energy system.

. . . identify energy guzzlers and emotional traps.

. . . plug the leaks.

. . . keep the energy tank "topped off."

. . . use your mind, rather than letting it use you.

. . . consciously choose the physical, mental, and emotional states you want to dwell in.

. . . co-create your reality.

To start with, how do you become aware of this energy system? How do you identify it or check its state of health? Where in the body is it situated?

Actually, the energy system doesn't exist "within" your body as you might imagine. *You* exist within *it*. It stretches out around you for an invisible radius of 16 to 30 feet. You're actually touching others' energy systems, absorbing much *from* them and giving much *to* them before you actually come into contact with them physically. In fact, you "sense" people's energy, feel the "vibes," respond to them, and bond with some more than others through this invisible process.

If you could look at the energy system, you would "see" that it surrounds you in multicolored layers. The first correlates to your physical body, the second to your emotional self, the third to your mental being, and so on. There are a total of seven layers, each of a higher vibrational frequency than the preceding one. Before you experience dis-ease, mental imbalances, or emotional disturbances, they actually show up in these bodies! So, if you can understand the interface between them and keep them "clean" and "uncluttered," you'll be able to increasingly choose states of wellness.

Some of the other systems in your body are easy to identify and "check out." You have a digestive system through which you take in food, use the beneficial portions, and eliminate the waste. It's quite easy to tell how efficiently this system is working. Similarly, you have a circulatory system that pumps blood all around your body. If it stops functioning even temporarily, your body panics and sends out clear warning signals. Likewise, the respiratory system is responsible for helping you breathe: for efficiently inhaling oxygen, sending it through the body, and exhaling the "waste." This, too, is a continual process, and if it were faulty, you would complain of congestion, shallow breathing, and other problems.

If any of these systems are in distress, laboratory procedures can help diagnose the cause. You can undergo tests to check out your stomach, intestines, bowel, and rectum. Electrocardiograms (ECGs) accurately tell you how your heart is beating. Other tests pinpoint how deep or shallow your breath is. X-rays show you graphic internal pictures of your "lung scape." Electroencephalograms (EEGs) monitor your brain.

How does the *energy* system exhibit itself, and in which laboratory can it be monitored? Through which tests can you gauge its state of health?

To give you a clue, the energy system is, in fact, "making its presence felt" almost every minute of your waking day. Sometimes you're aware of the movements of energy; at other times not. At still other times, you consciously choose to ignore them. On some occasions, you're caught in their grip, unable to manage them— they control you.

They vary in intensity, too. At one end of the spectrum, they can be gentle and soothing, exuding love and caring. At the other end, they can be loud and thunderous, destroying peace and stillness. And of course there are myriad shades in between. These movements of energy are rightly called *e-motions*. The *e* denotes energy: energy in motion.

Is there a laboratory test that can help you assess how your energy system is functioning? The answer is yes, and the test is a continual one: Your *emotions* are the gauge. And the laboratory is closer than you think . . . *it is your body.*

Chapter 2

GROWING UP

*"It is only human to trade
wholeness for approval."*

— RACHEL NAOMI REMEN, M.D.

Your body never lies. It's a very accurate "diagnostic center" for determining the state of your energy system. And it's the most easily accessible—it goes everywhere with you. It carries your entire historical record along, too! It constantly communicates with you through feelings and sensations. When you neglect, abuse, or overload your energy system, your body lets you know. As you'll see in the following chapter, it reaches out to you persistently and audibly and—with the passage of time—in an increasingly loud voice if you don't heed its warning signals in time. It's like the antivirus device on your computer, which flashes repeated warnings at you:

If you ignore them, it threatens, the whole system could crash! Such is the risk you run.

If you don't know how to listen to your body and decipher what it's trying to say, you're choosing to remain in the dark about vital clues that it's offering you.

One of the parameters in its "report" pertains to your emotional processing.

Let's go back to the beginning and see what emotional processing and other traits have been bestowed upon you at birth.

Newborn babies express themselves by crying. This is the first and most natural manner of communication, and children continue to use this method for the first few years. Whether wanting to be fed, cleaned, cared for, or comforted, they know exactly how to express their needs and get attention.

There's another enviable trait that they're gifted with at birth: *fearlessness*. In fact, there are only two fears they're born with: (1) falling, and (2) loud noises. What's often mistaken merely for ignorance is, in fact, an ignorance of *fear*.

A baby doesn't know she'll be burned if she touches a hot iron, nor does she know that it's not safe to put a finger into an electrical socket with the switch turned on. She's not afraid of the dark, no matter what her parents might assume—after all, she's been living in darkness and has felt quite safe there for close to nine months. She's probably surprised when her mother shouts "Cockroach!" and screams for help. To her, the cockroach—or any insect, mouse, or other living creature—is like a toy to be explored. When first introduced to the swimming pool, she's totally at ease in it, unaware that she could come to any danger at all in this "big bathtub." So it is with most new experiences: She naturally approaches each with wonder and curiosity.

She has been blessed with another rare quality: single-minded attention to whatever she may be doing. If she's playing with blocks, watch how she does so. Oblivious of anyone or anything around her, she focuses all her attention on balancing one on top of another. She feels each block—its angles, texture, color, and shape—as she carefully stacks it. She "experiences" each one. And the goal is just that. You realize that as you watch her play, when she carefully builds the tower, only to find it crash around her just as she had used up almost all of the blocks. Without the slightest trace of disappointment, however, she's back to building it, once again giving it her undivided attention. Obviously, the crash was only part of the game!

And while she's at it, what if she hurts herself? What if one day, on her "voyage of discovery" and in an unguarded moment, she falls or burns herself or gets frightened? She cries, of course. That activity, too, deserves her undivided awareness. When she's hurting, there's no room for anything else. When she howls, she gives it her all! You only have to watch her sob to know how wholeheartedly she does so!

And it's just the same when she's happy—or yearning for something. If she wants something, she wants it with all her heart, and she knows how to savor it when she gets it. She actually feels the pain or the pleasure *totally,* and then once it's over, she simply releases it. For example, once she has stopped hurting and has been tended to and received the love she needed, she's back to playing with abandon. In the evening does she remember that she fell or hurt herself earlier in the day? It's unlikely.

Honesty in every moment; a total, unashamed expression of self; an utter savoring of every experience: That's the child's way.

Have you ever wondered how that same spontaneous child becomes an adult who rarely cries, who finds it difficult to express her feelings, who is often so out of touch with herself that she doesn't even know *what* she's feeling? How does she become so full of fear and worry and lose that precious curiosity she was born with? Why does she find it so hard to ask for love? Why is it so difficult now to admit that she's hurting? Why does she feel unworthy and undeserving of love? Why does she think she has to work so hard to get approval? And where did that awareness, that 100 percent attention, go? Why is she so uncomfortable being in her own "space"? Why, above all, has she forgotten how to "be"?

Unfortunately, this is the process of growing up—the process of the outer world creeping in, almost insidiously, to dominate the inner one. It's a world of "shoulds" and "can'ts" and "shouldn'ts"—these compulsions become the rules for living.

The fearless baby learns caution. No doubt—this is useful, and she needs to protect herself. She certainly has to learn that an outlet plug isn't the safest place to explore, and she must find out that a hot iron will burn her. But along with that, she also absorbs many of the fears that the adults around her carry, most of them irrational. She may learn to distrust people . . . and circumstances, too. The atmosphere she's living in permeates her.

In fact, the process starts when she's still a baby. When she's upset or uncomfortable and cries, she senses her parents' discomfort. If she continues to cry, she often picks up on anger or irritation. Her calm and smiling face, on the other hand, earns her love and approval. These are the first "lessons" in adjustment. And what happens when she grows up a little more and begins to crawl and walk, and sometimes falls or hurts herself and expresses her emotions as she always did? A concerned mother rushes in, scoops her up, and more likely than not does one of two things:

1. "Nothing happened—don't cry," she says, dismissing the incident. In an effort to stem the flow of tears, she may perhaps add, pointing to the floor: "Look, an ant died where you fell!"

2. Or there's the promise of a usually forbidden "reward" to ease the pain: "chocolates" or "lots of ice cream." Distracted momentarily, the child stops crying.

What are the two messages here? Denial and/or distraction. *Be brave. Even if you're hurting, don't show it. Pretend it never happened—or at least assuage the pain with "pleasure."* These are powerful suggestions and become indelible rules for handling emotions in later life.

The rule changes subtly for boys: They're expected to be braver and more stoic, more in control than their sisters. Look how the pattern manifests later in life—how it is so hard for men to admit to stress, to talk about feelings, to cry, and to show how vulnerable they often feel. The opposite is true for women: They share their secrets with friends, shed tears more easily, and wear their "sensitivity" as a badge of honor.

One of the earliest emotions the child becomes aware of is jealousy. When she's two or three years old, she's told something that everyone seems very excited about, and it's an exciting new thought even for *her:* She's soon to have a baby brother. She doesn't quite understand what this means until a wailing bundle is brought home one day. Of course, the baby is quite a curiosity, but soon enough it seems he's crying constantly, attracting the attention of all the adults, especially their mother. The monopoly is gone! Now attention is divided between the two children and, so it seems to the older little one, sometimes quite unfairly.

She feels neglected and left out. She pinches her brother when she thinks that no one is looking. She becomes cranky and refuses to eat. If she could articulate her feelings, she might even say she "hates" this new arrival.

How many parents do you know who would validate this feeling and say something like: "I know you're feeling jealous. I can understand it. But I want you to know that I love you just as I always have. I always will, although of course I love your little brother, too." Instead, what the child is more likely to hear, uttered in incredulous tones, is: "You're jealous of your little brother? But he's so sweet!" Jealousy isn't an "acceptable emotion" to exhibit.

And there are others in a similar category—anger, upset, resentment, hurt, and fear are uncomfortable to deal with; these are emotions that should be hidden. Later in life, a mature person is a controlled person whose armor never slips to reveal any of these "vulner-abilities." There are additional rules of good behavior, too. Here are some of the things we've learned as we've grown up:

- Not to question
- Not to answer back
- To take care of others' needs before our own
- Not to cry when we're hurt
- To be brave under all circumstances
- Not to laugh too much
- Not to daydream

Depending on what a child's parents believe, she's subtly and subconsciously learning what it means to be a "nice person." Attitudes toward life, supposed axioms that will later on become self-fulfilling, and beliefs are all being indelibly imprinted on the impressionable little mind. She's receiving the first messages about herself and her capabilities. The groundwork is being laid for her lifelong sense of identity and self-esteem, as well as benchmarks for "maturity."

And then there are the "rules" about life and the best ways to live it. Of course, the messages may be vastly different: They could suggest sacrifice as a prime value, or individual fulfillment; they could uphold submission to another individual or imply just the opposite; they could communicate that the world is an abundantly stocked, friendly place and she'll always get what she wants, or they could prepare her for a tough and unfriendly world, packed with hostility: "Don't trust anyone—be careful." There are rules for everything she'll come into contact with: work, money, people, relationships, success, and love. These indelible rules become the bedrock for the child's behavior in later years: her "truths." They're the invisible parameters by which she measures every action.

And almost everyone in her life has a "message" for her: parents, grandparents, teachers, and—later—friends.

They are the pillars of her secure world, her emotional anchors. As such, their opinions are unquestionable. For the little child, they are the first rules of "survival." They tell her how it is acceptable to "be."

I can have a self or I can have
consistent behavior. I cannot have both.

— from *Notes to Myself,* by Hugh Prather

And so slowly, imperceptibly, like a sunflower turning to face its source of warmth, light, and growth, the child turns and turns and turns: trying to fit the patterns of conformity, to play by the rules of good behavior that she has been taught, and to adjust to circumstances.

Like the sunflower, by the end of the day, she has often turned 180 degrees. She no longer emotes naturally and without inhibition. She trusts her mind above her instincts, unlike her earliest responses. She has come to understand what gets approval, and she strives to earn it. She depends almost totally on external rather than internal validation. She smiles and smiles and dances and dances so that everyone can see that she's "in control." Those parts of herself that she thinks no one wants to see, she hides . . . even from herself.

And how or why do you think such obedience is enforced? There are two very important "weapons" that parents and other caregivers, as well as friends and—later— partners, have that can ensure conformity. They are something the child just can't do without—something we all crave even when we become adults: love and approval. To earn them, and then keep them, we'll do anything it takes.

Sometimes it takes a lot.

※　※　※

Chapter 3

THE COST OF
CONFORMITY

*"Biography becomes biology . . . we are all living
history books. Our bodies contain our histories—every
chapter, line, and verse of every event and relationship
in our lives. As our lives unfold, our biological health
becomes a living, breathing biographical statement that
conveys our strengths, weaknesses, hopes, and fears."*

— CAROLINE MYSS

The first thing we decide to do to be loved is to con-
form to all the rules of being "nice." Gradually, we begin
to display the "positive" emotions that win us approval
and hide the "negative" ones that earn castigation and
withdrawal of love. The latter are like naughty children:
often difficult to deal with, hard to manage, and not
very pleasant to have around. They're punished and sent
away until they've calmed down.

Now, managing negative emotions might not be a bad lesson to learn. In fact, you might imagine that such a lesson could hold you in good stead later in life. What's the harm if you're taught to be polite and considerate? And certainly, if you learned a technique that helped you hold your temper or release jealousy, hurt, or sadness, wouldn't you be acquiring a precious mechanism for survival? Well, unfortunately, no one teaches you that, and those unmanageable emotions don't just evaporate or vanish with time. Like punished children, they hang their heads and slink away in shame, but they don't disappear.

Other people in your life aren't the only judges whom you seek to hide them from. Within sits an even more stringent critic. You judge yourself, too, often even more harshly than others do. Do you want to show those around you what appears so "ugly" to your own eyes? Of course not. So you hide the "negative" feeling or disguise it behind another. Jealousy is a good example: It's the most difficult emotion to express to another person in a straightforward manner. So you complain, grow quarrelsome, and blame others. You become manipulative. You do the same when gripped by guilt—and in the case of many other similar emotions that might mar your image.

Apart from wanting to earn approval, there's another valid reason why we don't "feel" fully. Often at the time an event takes place it's very painful. To "save" ourselves, as a very justifiable defense mechanism, we put on a mask; get into control mode; and promise ourselves that later when we're alone, the feelings will find an outlet. But how often do we manage that?

Where do such "unfelt" emotions go? They have only one place to hide: in the body.

And this is how your physical self becomes that laboratory I spoke of earlier, which constantly processes your emotions and almost every moment is telling you exactly how motions of energy are entering and leaving your body. When they exit in love and trust, they make you feel positive. When they depart in fear and insecurity, you get negative "vibes."

If you choose not to accept the uncomfortable emotions, they sulk in some corner of the body. How do they choose this space? Is it random selection? Does it differ from person to person? Is the system genetic or hereditary? Do *you* choose the locations?

Does hurt, for example, go straight to the heart? What about worry? Does it travel to the head? Where does fear prefer to lurk? Or guilt? Resentment? Anger?

The magic of the system is that it's so beautifully engineered, so simply constructed, and so elegantly comprehensible that it seems a shame not to understand or be aware of it. It's the most amazing diagnostic tool you have to test how efficiently you're processing your emotions. It informs you when you suppress fears, hold on to hurts, repress conflicts, or are resistant to life's inevitabilities. Your mind may tell you all manner of comforting "untruths"; it may insist that you're undeterred by conflict or unaffected by stress and pressure. But your body will let you know *exactly* how well you're handling life.

So, how does your body communicate with you? In the only way it knows how to get your attention: by panging and aching and making you uncomfortable. To once again use the metaphor of the naughty child, this happens in gentle stages: At first, the child just asks you to give her what she wants. If you don't listen, her voice becomes more insistent. If you still don't heed it, she becomes aggressive and demanding. Finally, she throws a tantrum.

It's the same with pain: Initially, it's only a small discomfort; then it grows and expands its sphere. If it's still unattended to, it manifests itself more seriously. Finally, it becomes unmanageable. If you choose to live with it, you list it among your chronic ailments, usually attaching a possessive "my" whenever you mention it. Sometimes you stifle its voice with tablets, potions, and "healing" liquids. It's quiet for a while—but then, as soon as it senses the time is right and you're ready to listen again, it seizes its chance and speaks up.

> *"Illness can be seen as simply a message from your body to you that says, <u>Wait a minute; something is wrong. You are not listening to your whole self; you are ignoring something very important to you. What is it?"</u>*

— from *Hands of Light,* by Barbara Ann Brennan

Listen to what your body is attempting to say. Suppressed emotions, conflicts, fears, discomforts, and feelings of inadequacy don't hide in random places. In order to be able to "speak" to you directly and clearly, some part of the body becomes a "weak link," and its normal functioning gets disrupted. Here are examples (they might sound like generalizations initially, but pause and think a while and you might find some resonance in each statement):

- When there's something you don't want to "look at" clearly, something you're being near- or farsighted about, your eyes will bother you.

- When you don't want to hear clearly or when you're attempting to block out negative talk, criticism, or nagging, your ears will almost literally shut down.

- If you have trouble speaking up, difficulty expressing yourself, or are creatively blocked, you'll complain of chronic hoarseness or regular bouts of throat trouble.

- Your will to live is centered in your chest. Breath is life. If you ever feel suffocated by circumstances and are unable to "breathe," you'll notice respiratory problems or a "congested" chest. Asthmatics might confirm that an attack is often brought on by some such circumstance.

- The heart is the center of love and compassion. People who have had heart attacks might do well to add "Learn to give and receive love freely" to the list of the doctor's do's and don'ts. Forgiveness is the best cleansing "brush" for arteries clogged by hurt, bitterness, and resentments.

- When you're upset, anxious, or disturbed, the digestive system grumbles. Your inability to come to terms with the circumstances around you or your resistance to accepting reality actually causes indigestion. You're not able to take in nourishment or absorb it. Constipation is a sign that you find it hard to let go of what you no longer need—the waste emotions that no longer serve you.

- Anger hides in your liver, the organ responsible for producing digestive juices. Do *you* know of an angry person who "digests" life well?

- The pancreas is responsible for the balance of sugar in your body. Do you know what it does when you feel regret or perceive that there's not enough sweetness in your life? It "manufactures" sweetness. You're diagnosed with diabetes.

- Your thighs symbolize personal power and might demand your attention if you're feeling disempowered.

- Fears and criticism, with respect to yourself or others, affect your knees. So does inflexibility. The balance of the body rests on your ankles—lose it in life and you may well have to deal with pain or even a fracture in that delicate area.

- Discomfort in your calves or feet? Check out whether you're facing a dilemma or fear about where you're heading in life.

- The spine supports you. Every vertebra tells its own story. Generally, guilt and miserliness sulk in the middle, and financial insecurity in the lower back. Procrastinators might also suffer from dull aches, which will disappear once they make a to-do list and earnestly get down to work!

- Cervical spondylosis will be the bane of a rigid person, one who refuses to see both sides of a question. Or the vertebrae could be stiff with resentment, humiliation, and rejection.

- Responsibility is shouldered. If it's not borne with a sense of trust and joy, the burden will be "felt" by the shoulders.

Other ailments, too, have causes: Unresolved issues lead to high blood pressure. If they're very persistent, they turn into cancerous growths. Hardened resentment or even grief become stones in the gallbladder or kidneys. If you just refuse to let go, the bottled-up emotions get lodged in the organs responsible for the elimination of certain waste products: the kidneys. Repressed anxieties or other negative emotions erupt on the skin. Do you feel an excessive need to dominate and control? Do you think you can't flow with the tide? Gout might be the body's way of telling you to lighten up. A slipped disk manifests when you feel hopelessly unsupported and full of fear. With a more severe breakdown in structures, your bones literally give way—osteoporosis will be the diagnosis.

And these are only some of the signs. (For a more detailed study, see Louise L. Hay's book *You Can Heal Your Life*, Hay House, 2004.)

Language is so reflective, too:

- You *shoulder* responsibilities.
- A particular person can be a *pain in the neck!*
- You can't *stand* certain situations!
- Anxious? You feel *butterflies in the stomach.*
- Does someone get *on your nerves?*
- You find something *hard to stomach!*
- A situation is *hard to handle.*
- Fearful? You feel *weak in the knees.*

Do you say these things? Watch out—you might have pain in just these areas!

Isn't the system awe inspiring? The next time you feel physical discomfort, try to remember that it's not as random as it seems . . . nor is it caused just by sleeping in a particular way, or because of the weather. These might be contributory factors, too, but add to this your knowledge of the body-mind connection and you'll get the total picture. Sort out the conflict within, dropping the resistance and value judgments, and you can experience total healing. (I'll talk more about this topic in Chapter 8.)

As Eckhart Tolle, a well-known spiritual teacher and writer, succinctly puts it: "Emotion is where the body meets the mind."

So it is that the body, the channel for e-motions, is the most accurate gauge you could ever hope to find to measure what your mind "minds"! And thus your physical health is to a large extent dependent on the quality of your responses to life. This understanding is the key to lasting good health.

※ ※ ※

Chapter 4

ENERGY THIEVES

"The song that I came to sing remains unsung to this day. I have spent my days in stringing and in unstringing my instrument."

— RABINDRANATH TAGORE

Let's take a look at what keeps our energy system functioning cleanly, as well as what determines the quality of our responses.

There are some very obvious answers. Apart from physical necessities—food, rest, peaceful surroundings, and exercise—you could also add other elements that make you feel good: A beautiful sunset pulls you into the present moment; an inspiring piece of music transports you to a different plane; a walk in the deep silence of a forest helps you connect to your own Higher Self; and gazing into the clear, innocent eyes of a baby strips you of all masks and pretenses.

For these few blissful moments, you feel ecstatic, energized, and rejuvenated. In fact, that's just what these moments are: *energizers*. The more you're able to take breaks to experience them, the more you develop the capacity to savor every passing minute—no matter how seemingly ordinary—the better you'll feel. If, as the spiritual master Sri Sri Ravi Shankar advocates, you were able to turn every question into wonder, and if you could find cause for celebration in each moment, you'd have begun to discover the secret of the art of living.

Now let's suppose that you're fulfilling all the physical needs. You're eating right, sleeping well, exercising as you should, and even taking a few energizing breaks from your routine. Why do you still feel drained, joyless, and low on energy? Obviously, this isn't merely a physical phenomenon, then.

Each of us has been given the gift of life fueled by the life force or prana, an intelligent—some call it *divine*— energy. Why and how does this precious resource dwindle, sometimes to desperately low levels?

Certain emotions are energy thieves. What's worse is that it's daylight robbery! Not only do some of them make you feel miserable while you're experiencing them, but other more lethal ones can also trap you even when you think that you've tackled them effectively and can keep you imprisoned while they continue to drain you.

Worry

For many of us, worry is as natural as eating or sleeping. It's an imaginary screen onto which we project images of what can happen in the future. Unfortunately, the focus is only on things going wrong! Fear, doubt, and possible distress are built into these "mental pictures." We think about events that we're convinced are doomed to happen: Those who are ill won't recover; others who aren't already will fall ill; bad times will remain bad; good ones will take a turn for the worse; school-age children won't go to college; young adults won't find good partners . . . and, of course, potential mates might not turn out to be as good as we'd thought. In fact, as any worrier can tell you with conviction, since nothing in life is certain, obviously there's much space for conjecture!

For a habitual worrier, even situations that are currently favorable can change for the worse. It's therefore almost "responsible" to worry—it's a sign of caring! And most worriers attest to the fact that this activity becomes a habit. No sooner has one cause for doubt been banished than another is just waiting to occupy its place. There's always ample fuel for the fire of worry. And this is a greedy, unsatisfied blaze, always ready to devour more. It's a vicious story of burnout.

Think of what even a half-hour delay in a loved one's return can do to you. By the time the person walks in the door, you're feeling exhausted, weak, and ready to yell at—or even hit—him or her! It's like leaving a tap on: You have no reason to feel surprised when you see that the tank has no "water" left in it.

"Worry often gives a small thing a big shadow."

— Swedish proverb

What does this inference mean in energy terms? Consider this statement: *Energy follows thought.* So, as you continue to feed that fire—that is, as you're besieged by "negative thoughts" about all that may go wrong—you're actually "donating" energy to the very occurrences you wish to avoid. (I'll talk about this more later in the book.) As you continue to obsessively think about these events and imagine the consequences, energy continues to flow to them. Often you find them manifesting —a sort of negative wish fulfillment. And, of course, you declare that you "knew this would happen." Faith gets another nail in its coffin, and you believe you were justified to worry!

> *"Worry is a thin stream of fear trickling through the mind. If encouraged, it cuts a channel into which all other thoughts are drained."*
>
> — Arthur Somers Roche

Holding On to Hurt or Resentment

If worry drains you with fears of the future, then pain, resentment, and regret keep you chained to the past. As you "nourish" memories of people who have hurt you or let you down, of circumstances that haven't lived up to your expectations, and of unfulfilled dreams, your energy is actually being drained to something that can't be changed. Think about it: Somebody said or did something hurtful to you years and years ago. You can still remember and talk about this incident with tears in your eyes. The person may no longer be a part of your life and might even be dead, but you continue to leak energy to this thought.

*"Resentment is like taking poison and
waiting for the other person to die."*

— Malachy McCourt

Think of it this way: When somebody wants to hurt
you, imagine that he or she is actually throwing a stone
at you. The stone finds its mark and bruises you.

Let's assume that this happens before breakfast. Now
imagine that you've decided to spend that day doing some
of your favorite things. You're planning to see a movie,
have lunch at a new restaurant, and spend time with your
closest friend. While you're watching the film, perhaps
something on the screen reminds you of that incident in
the morning, and once again you feel the hurt. The bruise
is still there. Your mind goes back to it. You shift in your
seat as a wave of resentment flows through you. Then the
movie pulls you back into its story, and for a while you
forget the pain . . . but not for long.

As you tuck away your lunch and chat with your
friend, the wound reminds you once again of its presence. You tell your friend what happened, and she com-
miserates with you. Together you look at the bruise,
touch it, and feel it. It looks quite big, and it's beginning
to turn blue! You feel sorry for yourself. When you get
up and make your way home, you're feeling a delicious
validation of hurt, tinged with self-pity and spiked by a
firm resolve to neither forgive nor forget.

By the time the day comes to a close and perhaps you
meet up with whoever threw the stone at you, you're
sulking, upset, and eager to remind the person of his or
her error. You're waiting for an apology to "balance" that
energy drain. Whether you realize it or not, you have,
in fact, been leaking energy to the thought even while

you were supposedly enjoying yourself. Instead of feeling happy and rejuvenated, you're inexplicably drained by the end of such a day. Since you've also decided that you'll only lighten up once the other person validates your claim, you'll keep leaking this precious resource until that happens . . . if it happens at all.

Guilt

Guilt is one of the heaviest emotions and wears you out as you continue to carry it. We all make mistakes—sometimes serious ones—and upon realizing our folly, we feel regret or remorse. We hold ourselves culpable.

The problem arises when you can't let go of these emotions or—to put it differently—let yourself off the hook. You imagine that it would be irresponsible to be forgiven, so you internally condemn and rebuke yourself. Instead of coming to terms with your mistake and getting along with life, you continue to carry the burden. It's much like climbing a mountain with a large trunk on your back, a huge load that tires you and makes the journey seem unending. Your energy is sapped when you turn the harsh heat of blame on yourself. Self-esteem dips; you may become demanding and manipulative as you greedily seek from others the love and approval you refuse to grant yourself. You begin to wilt as you're no longer able to absorb the abundance surrounding you—you feel crushed.

Regret

Not everything in life happens just the way we want it to. Each of us holds dreams, expectations, and desires close to our hearts. Some mature; others don't. Thoughts of the latter often haunt us—or taunt us.

Let's look at this in a little more detail. Occasionally, regularly, very often, and then obsessively, you may find yourself returning to the past. You have two choices: (1) Reflect on it and accept it, or (2) attempt to rescript what has happened. The second option is obviously the one that's suffused with resentment and disappointment. A person gripped by regret knows that hours can be spent asking those impossible questions: *Why me? What did I do to deserve this fate?* or *Why is life so unfair?* No satisfactory answer is at hand, and the questioner will gradually slip into darkness, despair, or even depression.

Depression is actually akin to a huge pile of emotions bunched together like dirty clothes that no one wants to even look at, let alone wash. Indeed, their very existence is denied. Hurt, insecurity, and pain that seem overwhelming or threatening are blocked, deadened, and anesthetized by what's termed "depression." In fact, when you say that you're depressed, isn't that exactly how you feel? Somewhat dead, blocked to feeling, and numb: *de*-pressed—pressed down? Regret about how your life has turned out is often one of the major reasons for depression. Regret postpones life.

The regret may taunt rather than haunt. In that case, the emotion would be directed against yourself: *Why haven't I been able to control, manage, or fulfill the expectations of others or myself?*

If you recognize yourself in this pattern, you know how successfully you can undermine yourself and your self-respect. Even if the erosion is as gentle as water falling on a stone, very soon you'll develop a deep hollow of low self-esteem. And, of course, the water that will keep filling it will be murky with self-condemnation.

The so-called erosion is another word for the draining of energy.

Fear

Fear arises when you construct an imaginary reality. It's like playing a game of simulation in which you quite successfully forget that it's only a game! The characters are real, the situations even more so; the plot thickens as you watch, and the ending is usually unhappy. You can get a glimpse of the power of your mind in the way it evokes a fear and then holds you in its grip! Based on little evidence or by reactivating the trigger of a previous experience, the mind wondrously weaves a new scenario as it connives to convince you that the future will be similar to the past. Stop and think: *Is this necessary or true?*

Look at what the entire process does to you—it incapacitates you, paralyzes you, and makes you incapable of rational thought or action. How difficult it often is to switch off that endlessly playing movie that makes you feel weak and tremble at the knees.

Just visualize something that frightens you: the future, cockroaches, mice, airplanes, water, heights, or losing a loved one. As you imagine the entity, see if you can become aware of what happens in different parts of your body. Can you "feel" fear? Notice especially what happens to your heart, knees, solar plexus, and stomach.

In fact, the word *fear* itself is so beautifully reflective of the emotion. Have you ever wondered what the letters are an acronym for? F-E-A-R: False Evidence Appears Real. And anyone who has been in the grip of this emotion can testify to the "realness" of it all. Try telling a child—or an adult, for that matter—that there's nothing to fear in the dark and that an unlit room is empty and safe. The rational mind accepts this explanation, but eventually, fear triumphs.

Similarly, you can be totally trapped by a graphic picture of what the future will look like, presented to you by the camera that is your mind—in full color and vivid detail. If you're not careful, your mind can quite effortlessly convince you that this is the real picture. And as you might have realized by now, you would feel the effects on your body. Do you think such an experience would leave you feeling good or bad, energized or drained?

"He who fears he will suffer, already suffers from his fear."

— Michel de Montaigne

Grief

Sadness, sorrow, and the wrench of separation from a loved one are natural emotions. When you lose someone to death or the breakup of a relationship, it's bound to create a vacuum. You shift from feeling dazed or numb to intensely reliving memories to missing the person or even aching for him or her. Invariably, nature provides its own rhythm and a time frame for adjustment to the new reality. If there's a sense of shock, that, too, wears off after a while. But the point is, it *does*.

If you hold on to grief too long or too tightly, with no thought of ever letting it go, you're once more tying your energy system up in knots, which would be difficult to disentangle. As hard as it may be to accept, holding on to grief for the one who's gone isn't a "certificate of loyalty."

And just one more thought: Think of the person you've been separated from and honestly ask yourself what he or she would tell you to do under the circumstances—continue to grieve endlessly or get on with your life?

Do you know what it is exactly that prolonged grief does? It compels you to live as if you were half-dead. This emotion precludes you from acknowledging the gift of life.

*"Worry, doubt, fear and despair are the
enemies which slowly bring us down to the
ground and turn us [in]to dust before we die."*

— attributed to General Douglas MacArthur

Self-Pity

Falling into the deliciously dark well of self-pity is so easy—a small slip and you're in. It's a private space you choose so that you can be alone to lick your wounds and relive again and again the painful incident or past experience. You dredge up details of hurtful events and mentally replay the scenes, allowing yourself to wallow in them. Tear-jerking emotions, locked in with the incidents, resurface and have the power to transport you back in time. It's no coincidence that self-pity is described as a wave: It washes over you and, as it gets bigger and bigger, has the power to overcome you and take you out to sea, completely out of your depth and with no power to recover.

Self-pity leads to a tremendous drain on your energy, as you yourself should be able to acknowledge. Just consider how weak and exhausted you feel after a long spell of bitter crying or self-recrimination over an incident that you have no power to alter.

Jealousy

Jealousy is an acidic emotion that literally burns you up from the inside. Its closest ally is suspicion. Once these spidery emotions begin their activity, there's almost no letup. The two collude to tie you up in a web of misery. It is a chicken-and-egg story where it becomes impossible to decipher which comes first.

More than perhaps any other emotion, jealousy can blindfold you so totally that it's as if you're walking in the dark. Every "clue" is open to misrepresentation as your own understanding of reality moves further and further away from the truth. Finally, you find yourself alone, alienated and despairing. Unwilling to consider or even hear another point of view, this conniving emotion has the power to break hearts and relationships, often beyond repair. In addition, it can seriously threaten your sanity.

All of these emotions are quite, undercover workers. They wreak damage surreptitiously, and you sometimes don't even know about it until it's too late. Often, they're cleverly disguised or totally hidden. Self-sabotage is their mission.

One prominent emotion doesn't belong to this category, though. The emotion that's the subject of the next section is loud, often aggressive, boldly dressed, and ostentatious. When it wells up, it's hard to hide.

Anger

All the other emotions I've talked about involve only one person: you. However, anger is interactive; it involves others around you. In fact, it's directed outward and needs a target to fulfill itself.

Think of what happens when you're angry. For some reason, you feel out of control. Things aren't going the way you want them to. You feel helpless, impotent, and trapped. All these emotions well up within you—like lava erupting from a volcano, they surge up and spew forth, burning others around you. Everyone in the vicinity runs for cover; they agree to do whatever you demand.

Slowly the attack abates. Externally, things seem to have come under "control." You pacify yourself with the thought that the anger was justified and needed. You don't dare look inside yourself to analyze your feelings.

> *"If a small thing has the power to make you angry,*
> *does that not indicate something about your size?"*
>
> — Sydney J. Harris

Many of us who are prone to temper tantrums treat anger like alcohol: When it takes over, we say things we normally keep bottled up. We use it to hurt others and release pent-up feelings of desperation or frustration. Later, we attempt to dismiss our actions and statements because they were done or said under "the influence of anger."

Anger, because of the intense acrimony and heat it generates, has the power to wound and burn those around you. Within a very short time, it drains your energy, too, leaving you debilitated. Unfortunately, your outbursts tend to follow a pattern and, like the drink you crave, become addictive. Soon, you can think of no other way to be heard than by losing your cool. You begin to "lose it" more often and increasingly violently. Others around you, too, become immune to the milder attacks, so you have to resort to newer and harsher tactics to attract attention. That's certainly what you're seeking to "achieve" every time you lose your temper.

But anger is the symptom, not the cause, of the underlying malaise. It's like the temperature that shows up on your thermometer.

Have you ever wondered what *really* causes anger?

Make a list of the things that make you really angry. List them, and then grade them in order of priority.

Turn to Chapter 10 and see what really underlies these feelings.

All these emotions trap you. What does a trap feel like? Visualize an animal caught in a cage. It moves restlessly from one side to the other, desperately trying to find a way out. Even the food that originally lured it in ceases to provide any sustenance. As a result of fear and exhaustion, it finally dies.

When you're in the grip of one of these draining emotions, your state is no better. Lured by the bait, you, too, have gotten confined in a small, constricted space. You appear to be free, but you're not. You're as helpless and powerless as that animal in the trap. And you're losing energy by the second.

Do you know who or what tricked you into this trap?

It is your Ego.

※ ※ ※

Chapter 5

EGO GAMES

"What can a drop lose by getting into the ocean? It's an illusion that it is big. A drop thinks, 'I am great! I am so big—will I vanish?' You will vanish if you don't unite with the ocean."

— SRI SRI RAVI SHANKAR

Ego is a much-misunderstood word. We commonly think of the Ego or of egotistical people as being proud, arrogant, and unmindful of others' feelings—maybe even brash and uncaring. This isn't what I'm referring to here. The Ego in the context of these pages is the totality of the conditioned mind: our personality . . . all the components of who we've become in order to exist in society.

We've seen how this happens. In Chapter 3, I discussed how a carefree child, uninhibited and fearless to start with, becomes bound by societal rules, regulations, norms, and mores of behavior and acceptability.

So what has really happened here? She started off life innocently, emoting from the heart, saying and doing exactly what she felt. Slowly, involuntarily, the mind started to take over.

That isn't to say that this is undesirable. Each of us needs the mind to interact with the world, to process information, to collate and interpret it, and to coordinate our life and the numerous activities it entails. The regret isn't that we learn to use the mind to do all this; it's that we actually allow it to completely dominate us, thereby stifling feelings, intuition, and wonder.

We become conditioned to trust only our "thinking," which is the product of the logical, left part of the brain. We tend to be bound by black-and-white definitions and judgments, which have to be supported by scientific evidence. We begin to believe that the only way to be is to *control:* ourselves, others, and Life itself. What happens, then, to feelings, hunches, higher wisdom, and insights that defy logic and factual proof? Where does the sense of curiosity and fun go? What becomes of the natural flow? What happens to trust in Life itself?

We choose to smother them. We begin living within a highly contracted paradigm, ignoring another vast potential available to each of us.

❧

Your personality is a contrivance to help you cope with the rest of the world. When you were born, it was absent. Babies and small children have no defined sense of self or identity. You might have noticed that until they're about age three, children refer to themselves in the third person! Then slowly, as it's time for them to enter school, it becomes necessary to create the barriers and personal boundaries that will protect them. And so it is that the Ego or sense of self or personality begins to take shape.

You begin to believe that the only way you can remain safe and protected is by distancing yourself from others. With time, this personality solidifies. Varied beliefs and experiences reinforce it. It develops certain set ways of responding and functioning vis-à-vis others.

We all develop our own sets of likes and dislikes. Each of us has different parameters of judgment. We each carry invisible lists of expectations and beliefs. The Ego is like the secretary who takes notes and reminds us of them in each situation. When something or someone "matches" up on the like/dislike chart or fulfills the expectation we hold, the Ego is content. If the scenario is reversed, the Ego gets ruffled. It won't let things be. It rises up to "protect" us, the boss, feeling that it's doing its duty. It shows us the entire file on the subject in question! It has a long and very efficient memory, and it's not content until the situation has been redressed and settled to its satisfaction.

The word *mind-set* is very illustrative. It's extremely difficult to move from the set position we've adopted. Habits, patterns in relationships, our perceptions and attitudes . . . all restrict us.

"We don't see things as they are. We see things as we are."

— attributed to Anaïs Nin

How does all this show up in real life? Visualize this scene: A young couple is having an argument. With tears in her eyes, the woman is recounting how hurt she's feeling over a remark her husband made a few days ago. His explanations don't appease her. "But how could you have said that?" she asks again, looking at him reproachfully.

As she continues to complain and accuse, he gets into the momentum of the game, too. Defensively, he reaches back into the past, to another time when she let *him* down. Taking the cue, she quotes something unforgivable that his mother said months ago. He reminds her how badly her brother behaved. Their voices rise, tears flow, buried resentments break loose, both don hostile armors, and the match begins in earnest. You can well imagine the unhappy climax.

How many players can you see in this scene? Two, of course. But can you recognize some invisible players: the loyal "secretaries" on both sides, each wanting to "win the match" for his or her own side and egging on the players to continue the blame game? See how they step in and take over. And notice how they then start to control the game, including its momentum and conclusion. If you could look inside each person after he or she has finished arguing, you'd see that the "game," thanks to the Ego, continues within. New evidence is dredged up as the highlights of the match are replayed and "improvements" planned for the next round.

You can replace the players with a father/son pair, a boss and an employee, close friends, siblings, or a mother and daughter, but the scenario will essentially remain the same.

It's interesting that all emotions emerge from two basic sources: love or fear. Now, if you look at the preceding scene, where do you think the emotions of both players are coming from? From spaces of vulnerability, blame, and insecurity: In other words, they arise from a basic fear. Hurt is evident, and so is defensiveness. Both parties are being judgmental and accusing. Suspicion and doubt creep in. Trust exits. It becomes all-important to be proven right. Pain surfaces; self-pity takes over. All these are Ego spaces. They're all low-energy states, where love can't find a toehold. For the moment it has been forgotten, banished.

Isn't it funny how we "protect" the Ego and its subversive activities? It's almost like the collusion of a victim with an abuser; we "hide" the event.

Imagine this scenario: You feel jealous. You could recognize this as an Ego-induced state, which it certainly is. You could bring it right out into the open and declare that this is how you feel . . . but is that what you habitually do? Most likely, you justify the emotion; you're unaware that you're being manipulated and alienated and thus manage to fall right into the trap. The same happens with hurt, rejection, fear, or resentment. The Ego remains safe and hidden, which is how it loves to be. Try declaring *it* to be the guilty party instead of your partner and see what happens!

It's clear, then, that when the Ego is in control, you . . .

. . . feel hurt and may choose to remain so.

. . . can only see your own point of view.

. . . have no desire to "make up."

. . . are very determined to enforce what you think is right.

. . . are unable to forgive or let go.

. . . are unable to accept unfulfilled expectations.

. . . are often cut off from feeling "softer" emotions such as love, vulnerability, gratitude, and joy.

. . . feel a sense of separation from those you love.

. . . feel alienated and uncared for.

. . . are often gripped by emotions like distrust, fear, insecurity, worry, and regret.

. . . are unable to accept and flow with life as it is.

Think of the relationships in your life. If there's discord, isn't it because of one of these reasons? In fact, call to mind any situation that makes you miserable. Don't you feel so bogged down that no resolution seems possible? You begin to think that there's no choice.

The reason behind each miserable situation is the Ego. But is there *really* no choice?

Look at that same husband-and-wife example, but let's imagine what love would do if it were allowed in. To start with, the husband could decide to listen to what his wife is saying. He might need to explain that he never meant to hurt her and is sorry that he did. If he were to do that, the play would end right then . . . and quite differently. There would be no more recriminations. The couple would probably end up having an intimate chat about their inner feelings, possibly over dinner at a quiet restaurant. It would be an opportunity for a deepening of their relationship.

The two emotions I spoke of, love and fear, emanate from two different centers of inner guidance. One voice tells you to trust, the other is skeptical; one voice tells you to flow, the other restrains you; one voice urges forgiveness, the other retribution; one joins, the other alienates. One is the voice of your Higher Self, the other of the Ego. One is the voice of the heart, the other of the conditioned mind or personality. One suggests an expansive paradigm, the other a contracted one. One enhances your energy, the other drains it. You don't need to guess which is which.

> *"The ego urges you to accomplish, while the soul merely asks you to enjoy the process."*

— Doreen Virtue

Why, then, don't we always choose the second outcome? Actually, sometimes we feel powerless—"energyless" might be a more accurate description. In such a state, it's often difficult to choose a happy ending.

When you're in the grip of the Ego, you feel joyless, stressed, cranky, and irritable. Your immunity is low. You feel alienated from others, even though, upon reflection, you find that it is *you* who doesn't feel like reaching out or communicating. Your relationships suffer as you become increasingly insecure, possessive, and manipulative. Your self-esteem dips as you grow less confident and are unable to cope even with daily tasks. You're unwilling to proffer love or forgiveness—and, on your end, you desperately need love, but no matter how much someone gives you, it never seems to be enough!

All these are signs that your energy system is cluttered.

However, even though that's how it may seem, the Ego isn't your enemy. It's behaving in the only way it has been trained. It can be a valuable ally, giving you a sense of self and healthy confidence. But if you're unaware of your true feelings or are feeling low, the Ego finds it easy to dominate you. You're unable to control it and tell it to stop playing games. It's an innovative and persistent game creator, too. So if you follow it, you can very quickly find yourself in an endless labyrinth.

The letters of the word *Ego* define it aptly: E-G-O— Energy Goes Out. And when energy is lost, your ability to cope with your predicament or choose wiser ways of handling things is further reduced.

There's one major factor that either encourages or discourages the role the Ego plays . . . it's the quality of your mind, the seat of the Ego. A noisy, restless, and agitated mind provides fertile ground for the Ego seeds to blossom and grow. A quiet mind, in contrast, encourages the Higher Self to be heard and followed.

Chapter 6

THE MOBILE MIND

"The human condition: lost in thought."

— ECKHART TOLLE

We're living in the age of the mobile phone. The following example must sound familiar: A ring tone beeps when you're watching a movie in a theater, urgently pulling you away from what's happening on the screen. You can't resist answering. By the time you've gone outside and finished your conversation, you've lost the thread of the story.

You've barely settled down when the vibrating alert buzzes, informing you that you have a text message. You tell yourself that you'll only look at it. You do. But soon you're hooked. You have to respond, if only to say that you're at the movie theater. The writer messages you back, telling you to get in touch with him or her as soon as you're free. You decide to send another message asking anxiously if the matter is very urgent.

And so the game continues, dragging you out of the theater at random junctures. This scenario could be repeated at a restaurant where you're out to dinner, at a child's school function, or at a business meeting. That ring, that beep, that buzz has the power to pull you out and away from whatever activity you happen to be involved in.

Your mind is like that mobile phone. No matter what you may have chosen to do, it beeps, buzzes, and vibrates to remind you of other things: to "message" you about random occurrences or to pull you out of the present moment to the past or future. Its messages can thrill you; excite you; or make you joyful, restless, or anxious. Once your mind is on—and it always is—you find its magnetic power hard to resist. Rarely do you realize how little control you actually exercise over it. *The reality is that you've become its slave.*

Here is a comical example: While I was watching a movie, my cell phone, seemingly on "silent" mode, buzzed with a message. What I just now described happened. A number of messages flew up on-screen. Finally, I had to leave the theater for a few minutes to answer an insistent caller. I came back and settled down again. It seemed inexplicable, but in the few minutes I'd been out, the hero, who had been poor and miserable, seemed to have suddenly had a stroke of luck. Now he was living in a mansion, surrounded by luxuries. Well, such "miracles" aren't uncommon in Indian movies! I continued to watch, although with some incomprehension. When I spoke to my friend about it, she burst into laughter and incredulously asked: "But don't you know—the original hero died and was reincarnated?!"

This isn't a commentary on Indian movies, but on how your mind can completely whisk you away from where you are so that you miss out totally on the reality of the present moment. And, unfortunately, it goes everywhere with you—your mind, I mean!

I often hear people say that they've been through a very stressful time and are going to take a break from their routine: a vacation to some beautiful location. Such a change would be very beneficial. But you know that you can ruin even the most idyllic plans, because while you may be physically there, mentally you're far, far away! The scenic mountain resort you've chosen to go to is tranquil and lovely. The fragrance of the pines invites you outside. The snowcapped mountains appear from behind the veil of clouds after days of hiding. The air is crisp and clean.

But where are *you?* Arguing with a friend who has hurt you; sitting at the bedside of a sick loved one, anxious and fearful; still at your office desk, biting your nails with worry over missing a deadline; or at home wondering if everything is safe and "under control"! It may come as a surprise to you that you're not where your body is—you're where your *mind* is. Only when the mind and body are in the same place are you in the present!

To be fair, though, both the cell phone and your mind have their advantages, too. You can use your phone to allay fears at home if you're running late or to call for help when your car breaks down; it's certainly a wonderful aid when you need to summon an ambulance. Actually, that's what it is meant for. But this device has insidiously overstepped its bounds: Dr. Jekyll has become Mr. Hyde.

And it's the same with your mind. It's a wonderful tool with a variety of uses. You can rely on it when you need to analyze complex data, to plan a project, to invent something new, or to seek solutions to knotty problems. You're supposed to be the boss who "switches it on" when it's needed, uses it, and then promptly switches it off.

As with your cell phone, how often do you manage to do that? Consider how agitated and helpless you feel if your phone runs out of battery power, is lost, or is left behind at home. In fact, you let *it* use *you*. You feel uncomfortable when you're asked to switch it off. You begin to feel shaky and disoriented without it.

Even if you decide to make time to connect with yourself, you can't manage to switch *your mind* off. At the most, you put it on "silent mode," which means that it appears to be quiet, but in actuality all activities continue! If you sit down to meditate, for example, it reminds you that this is a nonproductive activity, a waste of time. If you're reading or relaxing, it interrupts you with other distracting thoughts. It effectively uses doubts, fears, and worries to keep you agitated. Even when you're sleeping, it has the power to wake you, and as soon as it has your attention, it kicks in cleverly with whatever it knows will keep you up and under its control.

Like the cell phone, the mind has no powers of discretion to determine which messages are important and which aren't and which need to be delivered and which don't. It's simply greedy, anxious to grab your attention and keep it. It's happiest when your dependence on it becomes total, when it knows that you just can't do without it.

"This is the situation of your head: I see cycle-handles and pedals and strange things that you have gathered from everywhere. Such a small head . . . and no space to live in!"

— Osho

Consider how your mind can keep you imprisoned. Think of something that has been bothering you lately. Whether it's a business deal, a venture that has hurt you, anxiety about some perceived problem, a fear of losing something, anger over being betrayed, the loss of a job, or the end of a relationship, do you realize how obsessive your thoughts are about the issue in question?

Your mind, driven by the Ego, will just not let go. As soon as you seem to feel a modicum of relief, the mind will start acting up again, coming up with new ramifications and complications. Hours can pass without your realizing what exactly is taking place. And the mind sometimes needs no more than a single thought to keep you in a state of anxiety. Like one mosquito persistently buzzing around a room, it can drive you crazy! You feel miserable, stressed, hopeless, and drained. Unlike the mosquito, which can be swatted, you don't *try* to get rid of your impinging thoughts! Rarely can a solution emerge from such a situation.

What's still more amazing is that you don't even have control over which thoughts are going to pop into your mind or when! They can be triggered by a fragrance, a memory, an image, a random line in a newspaper or book, or a photograph. Or just like that . . . they don't need a trigger at all! Do you realize how the mind can instantly shift your mood?

Consider the following scenarios:

- You're listening to some melodious music and enjoying yourself one moment, yet the next, you can suddenly go into the "wronged" or recrimination mode.

- You're driving peacefully along a shady, traffic-free road. A disturbing thought about your child or partner—or anyone, for that matter—can reduce you to a bundle of anxiety.

- You're in a deep sleep, but you can awake suddenly in a cold sweat.

And, of course, most of the thoughts would be negative. We seem to be more easily hooked to that variety—and more susceptible to believing them, too! It's very seldom that we sit down to relive some pleasant moments from the past! We take for granted that things can and will go wrong. We're suspicious of joy. That, again, is how we've been conditioned, and the mind has learned the lesson well.

Have you ever thought about how disobedient and capricious your mind is about time? You're enjoying yourself; you're with your loved one—now time seems to fly! You're sitting in class listening to a boring lecture . . . it seems to drag on. You're waiting at the airport or railway station for someone to arrive: Every minute feels like an hour. When you want the mind to make time expand, it forces it to contract! When you want something to end, the mind stretches it out to infinity! But can you do anything about it?

"When a man sits with a pretty girl for an hour, it seems like a minute. But let him sit on a hot stove for a minute and it's longer than any hour. That's relativity."

— Albert Einstein

Did that movie with its story of reincarnation sound far-fetched? Our real lives and what we do to ourselves in a matter of moments are perhaps more so!

I feel the saddest when I meet people who say that they have it all—comfortable surroundings, good health, and "great" partners or children or bosses—yet they're unhappy. Why?

Have you seen a pearl ensconced in an oyster? The shell in which it's enclosed is its universe. The ocean stretches all around, filled with wondrous miracles, but the pearl only knows its small shell. Is it even aware that there could be a bigger picture? No. It's quite content in its confined paradigm where everything revolves only around itself.

If you're living a life dominated by the Ego and its whims, you, too, are like that pearl: beautiful, no doubt, but enclosed in the shell of your mind and unaware of the vastness around you!

※ ※ ※

Chapter 7

BEING HAPPY: IS IT A CHOICE OR A MATTER OF CHANCE?

"If you want to be happy, be!"

— HENRY DAVID THOREAU

It appears to be a dismal scenario: a labyrinth set up to make it impossible for you to reach the center.

The mind, without your permission, bombards you with thoughts, many of them unpleasant. The Ego abets the process. The thoughts give rise to emotions—some of them disappear, but others remain to plague you for years on end, draining you of energy like invisible leeches. They cause you pain, which then settles in your body as a chronic dis-ease.

Or, maybe this scenario doesn't apply to you. You feel that you're self-managed and self-controlled and remain peaceful unless others around you upset or provoke you or life situations become bothersome. *That* wrecks your peace.

Are you doomed to remain in these cages? Like that desperate animal (which I described in Chapter 4), are you going to run from one end of the trap to the other, only to finally give up?

Think about the answers to the following questions:

- Is being happy a choice?

- As you wake up, can you choose your state or mood for the day?

- When you say that all you really want is peace of mind, what do you really mean?

- How and where do you get such peace?

If I were to ask you whether these things were up for grabs—whether, in fact, it was possible to live happily ever after—what would be your answer? I've posed this question to many people, and most of the answers I've received have been in the negative. Living happily ever after happens solely in fairy tales, I'm told, and that, too, only occurs at the end of the story! We don't really know what happens next. How can we live happily "ever after"? Living happily ever after is an illusion. It's dependent on so many things—how can we be sure that they'll all happen?

There *is* uncertainty, of course, since most of the things we desire lie externally, and we seem to have no control over when and how they'll come to us. For many of us a satisfying job with a rising career track, money, status, and material markers symbolize "happiness." Some of us place a premium on relationships. How much approval, validation, and recognition we receive from those around us determines how contented we feel. At other times, we focus on certain "wishes" coming true.

Of course, there's no harm in wanting dreams to manifest, in nurturing expectations, or in desiring all manner of comforts and luxuries. You probably experience a great feeling of well-being and abundance when the goals you've set are achieved, expectations met, and desires fulfilled.

But what happens when your plans go awry? If your sense of well-being stems *only* from that external wish fulfillment, obviously you'll feel extremely upset, hurt, and miserable. Your graph of happiness will dip or soar according to circumstances, the behavior of others, your expectations, and your likes and dislikes. If everything is going according to plan, you'll feel satisfied and joyful. When you encounter a hurdle or things fall apart, as they're sometimes wont to, you'll feel troubled.

"A great trick to getting what you want, fast, though one requiring a deep level of understanding, is 'insistence.' Not the kind, however, that expects 'life' to behave a certain way, but the kind that expects you to behave a certain way."

— from *Notes from the Universe:* **www.tut.com**

If you paused and thought about your life right now and maybe gave it a title, what would it be? How do you feel about your life? Can you sum it up in a single word? Is it a happy or unhappy one? Do you feel that life hasn't given you your due—that it has been unfair and cheated you? If you do, you might even feel irritated that I've asked you this question.

Suppose that you've been diagnosed with a debilitating illness, lost a loved one, or been jilted or otherwise betrayed . . . what can you possibly do about such a situation other than being upset? Suppose somebody has rejected you, treated you unfairly, or humiliated you; wouldn't it be an expression of weakness on your part if you didn't feel affronted and justifiably angry? And if the person who has caused all the distress also happens to be a loved one, someone you've done a lot for, don't you have a right to feel sorry for yourself?

In these circumstances, what choice do you possibly have? How can you hope to be happy if the circumstances are not?

Well, if your understanding is that circumstances create your state, then of course, you're right. You can't hope to be content if everything around you isn't as you desire. As long as you believe this, you'll regularly feel helpless, trapped, powerless, lost, victimized, and resentful. You feel victimized when your capacity to cope seems dwarfed in comparison to the circumstances you're faced with. You feel "small" and powerless; the situation appears to be big and menacing.

What do you do when you feel defeated? Do you blame others, keep on complaining, and feel sorry for yourself? If the answer is yes, then you're living in a disempowered state in which you're certain that you're a victim of circumstances.

Blaming and complaining are typical responses. Even if a glass of water falls off a table, the first reaction is to question who placed it at the edge! You also grumble about how careless people are. So, if someone or something upsets you, most of your energy is focused on faulting the person or circumstance and then perhaps getting into the intricacies of how the goof-up could have happened! This, too, indicates a victimized state, and you can stay trapped in it forever.

You're a victim when you're a prisoner to your past. You feel betrayed and let down by circumstances, people, and perhaps Life itself. Energetically, you're wounded and bleeding. Your life force is leaking away into a pool of self-pity. Obviously, you'll feel joyless and drained. The past can't be changed, and if you refuse to leave it where it belongs—in the past—you'll carry it along into the present and future. Burdened with it and expecting it to repeat itself, you'll allow it to steal your present as well as your future from you. You'll allow the very people or circumstances "cheating" you to continue to repeatedly "abuse" you.

Here's another typical setup for remaining victimized and miserable: You feel sure that *everything* can be resolved if only a particular person changed his or her behavior. You're convinced that this will make adverse circumstances vanish, and things will work out the way you're hoping. You yearn for such a change in behavior.

But in spite of the fact that the solution seems so simple and so obvious—at least to *you*—you can't force it to come about. You feel hopeless, impotent, misunderstood, and unhappy. And you can remain that way for quite some time, believing that it's *the only solution*. Your life remains on hold. If you leave it to others to ensure your happiness, you might very often be disappointed. This, too, is a disempowered state.

You're using external circumstances—situations or another person's behavior (an uncertain entity)—as a justification, a crutch, to remain miserable. You've allotted a greater significance to another person's behavior, opinions, and attitude than to your own "right to be happy." You've agreed to allow those factors to "steal" your peace of mind at this moment, deciding that until they change, you'll remain miserable. By depending on something totally out of your control to make things better for you, you're on tenuous ground.

There's another scenario you can consider: When something untoward happens, have you ever caught yourself thinking or saying, "I have to live with it"? Perhaps this appears to be an acceptance of the reality, a statement that you've coped capably and dealt with the situation satisfactorily. But reconsider: Your response has resignation and defeatism built into it. It's a tired and listless statement that throws up an image of a person carrying a heavy load with no chance of ever putting it down. Loss can take time to recover from, but is it a burden that you have to carry forever?

How do you recognize a disempowered state? Here are some possible pointers:

- You feel unable to cope with the situation.

- You believe your misery can be alleviated only if the circumstances change.

- You constantly seek an energy "balance" from an external source.

- You feel drained, depleted, and dependent.

- You dwell in self-pity.

- You manipulatively seek love, affirmation, and validation from others.

- You're low on self-esteem.

- You're imbalanced, moody, and demanding.

- You manifest sickness to get sympathy.

- You're bad company!

Is there any other way you can get out of this state? I believe that there is. Ponder the epigraph at the beginning of this chapter and then decide for yourself your course of action.

"What is the meaning of life? To be happy and useful."

— H.H. The Dalai Lama

Consider this statement: *Circumstances don't define the quality of your life; your response to them does.* You can't control or change the "externals" in your life. The only part you do exercise some control over is the "internals": your mind, thoughts, and emotions. No matter what the stimulus, you still have the power, if you wish to acknowledge it, to choose how you respond and how much "power" or significance you allot to those external situations.

You can choose to react with hatred and bitterness at one end of the scale, or with love and gratitude at the other. And there are numerous shades in between. You can leave it to others to "fix" things for you, or you can begin right away to fix how you *feel* about things. You can choose to hold on or let go. It is *the latter choice* that decides your level of happiness, contentment, peace, fulfillment . . . call it what you will.

*"The state of your life is nothing more than
a reflection of your state of mind."*

— Dr. Wayne W. Dyer

Even if you've chosen to take responsibility for yourself and live in an empowered manner, you, too, may feel upset, let down, or anxious—but not for long. You'll become aware that you're falling into an unnecessary trap and will snap right out of it. Instead of blaming others around you, you'll see that it's your mind and Ego that have temporarily gripped you. Perhaps you're depleted energetically and thus have allowed this to happen. You'll focus now on getting balanced within so that the external situation, no matter how troublesome, ceases to irk you.

In fact, you'll realize that it's this state of energy itself that determines how you perceive the circumstances in the first place. When you're in a positive state, big "calamities" appear insignificant. When you're not energetically fit, even small incidents upset you. In a low-energy, victimized state, you can't help but minimize the good and magnify what's wrong—the focus remains outside. In an empowered state, you can effortlessly minimize "externals," focus on what's going well, and concentrate on further strengthening the *internal* center of power, the only one you can really depend upon.

Do you remember the traffic-jam examples I brought up at the start of the book? You can choose to be any of those three travelers: the first, who is very angry; the second, who is agitated but later calms down; or the third, who is peaceful and unfazed. Do you realize that your response would determine the quality of your life? In other words, you can be as "happy" or "unhappy" as you choose to be.

This realization can be very liberating, and if you feel a thrill of excitement or hope as you read this book, you're taking the first step of a highly rewarding journey. It's one that will enable you to become empowered rather than remaining a victim. Until now, you may have felt that you were at the mercy of circumstances and the people around you, not to mention Life in general and even the quality of your mind.

You can make a paradigm shift right now by taking your power back from all the places where it has been scattered. First of all, allow the understanding to seep in that that external power, which supported you, is an unfaithful mistress and can't be relied upon. Real power, real stability, and real security lie within you; and perhaps you've never even looked at them.

Replace external striving for control with inner "response-ability." Stop blaming and stop complaining. Let go of what no longer serves you. Take charge of your life, and accept that you've created all the circumstances you find yourself in. Assume responsibility for your state of physical, mental, emotional, and spiritual well-being and give up the burden of manipulating all the circumstances and situations you face!

Each of us has had to face hardships, disappointments, and sorrows in our lives. What have *you* chosen to become under pressure? A piece of coal or a diamond? Coal—raw carbon—blackens everything it touches. It's hard to wash off. It breaks under pressure. A diamond shines quietly, casting a beautiful spell on all who gaze at it. It gets *polished* by pressure.

And it's never too late. Decide . . . choose to become the diamond you were always meant to be.

✸ ✸ ✸

Chapter 8

A NEW PARADIGM

"There is only one journey.
Going inside yourself."

— RAINER MARIA RILKE

Of course, you might very well say, "I want to be free, empowered, in charge of myself, and happy no matter what; I want to be the shining diamond." Who doesn't? The question, then, is: *Why haven't you chosen to do and be so?*

And the answer might be one of the following:

1. "I didn't know I had a choice."

2. "Being a 'victim' is easier. It's comfortable. It's the only way I know, and change is scary. When people push my buttons or Life does

> so, I mechanically react in the same old way
> I'm used to. A new way of being—like any
> new skill—requires practice, alertness, and
> awareness. I'm not sure I want to do it."

Actually, each of us has a comfort zone, a place where we feel "safe." The security is largely provided by familiar patterns of thinking, perceiving, and behaving. Changing any of these patterns is obviously uncomfortable. Resistance crops up—the Ego provides the relevant excuses. It would feel out of control if we chose to grow or seek empowerment, so it fights and kicks to hold on.

When you choose a path of personal growth or empowerment, an internal battle rages. One part wants to move; the other wants to remain where it is. The secret is to understand this dichotomy and to focus energy not on the triggers that push your buttons but on the internal resistance.

The "old space" allows you to be dependent. It shifts the onus for your happiness onto others. And of course, such a state of affairs has its advantages. It gets you sympathy, from others as well as yourself. You can "shirk" some of your responsibilities, too, because you feel depressed or sick or miserable. Being at someone's mercy, pushed around helplessly by the twists and turns of fate, sanctioned to wallow in the well of self-pity, could evoke a delicious feeling. To complain about others, especially if you're fortunate enough to have attentive listeners, is equally gratifying.

How would it feel if you now vowed never to curse fate or complain about the people in your life? Imagine if you were never afforded time to worry, fear, or doubt. Imagine if you undertook to always live in a state of trust, faith, and surrender. It all seems unrealistic.

*"Take your life in your own hands and see what
happens? A terrible thing: no one is to blame."*

— Erica Jong

Does it shake you to know that you can't hold anyone except yourself responsible for your misery? Do you wonder how you'll cope without blaming a boss who makes your life hell, a spouse who dominates you, a friend who betrays you, a parent who puts you down, or a child who neglects you? Surely you're "entitled" to feeling misunderstood, low, and unhappy?

Well, of course—as a temporary situation. But do you really want to carry that burden all your life? Are you okay with letting it pollute your present? Are you willing to let it snuff out the joys that each new day holds? Are you willing to allow others to have total power over the quality of *your* life? If you continue to be an "irresponsible victim," that's what you'll be doing.

How do you break out of this viselike grip? The first step is having the willingness to see another paradigm—another perspective—and consider another way of being. The second is making a clear intention to follow the new path. The Universe (that is, a Higher Force, what people refer to as God) does the third step for you. It is *Grace:* the propeller that gets you moving on this path.

Very few agree to give up time-tested, comfortable, and habitual ways of behaving just because they read that it's possible or listen to an inspirational lecture. If you did *that,* it would be one of the demonstrations of Grace. The rewards of empowerment are a feeling of being in charge, confident, and free. The price you have to pay is giving up a comfort zone: a habitual way of thinking, behaving, and perceiving.

Most of us require a push to get us started.

Those of us who have managed to trap ourselves rigidly in an armor of Ego need a hit to break it open and even accept that there's another way of approaching life. The "hardness" of the hit would be determined by the "hardness" of the armor!

So, Grace comes in unrecognizable packages! Things may start to go "wrong." A terminal illness is suddenly diagnosed. A bad investment leads you to financial ruin. The breadwinner of the family suddenly passes on, leaving you unprotected and helpless. The most significant relationship in your life breaks down. You lose a job and the sense of power and security it afforded you. You feel helpless, angry, betrayed, and totally beaten. Actually, primarily, you feel out of control—the control you feel only *you* wield in your life. Now suddenly things seem to be slipping out of your grasp. They're not going the way you'd foreseen. You question life and circumstances. It's a dark, despairing time.

External circumstances, or even internal ones, could cause this state of affairs. You can bring yourself to a similar point of joylessness by allowing the Ego to completely dominate your life—as I've said, it's usually demanding and not easily satisfied. You feel forced to give in to its whims. Gradually, you notice that you're becoming increasingly rigid and inflexible. You need to always be right and have your way. To achieve this, you become judgmental and controlling. You start throwing tantrums.

Simultaneously, you set still higher goals for yourself. You work longer and harder. By amassing achievements, you try to fill the yawning void caused by unfulfilling human interactions. The walls of your prison become higher and more impenetrable. The cell darkens. Insecurity increases. The feeling of emptiness within deepens. The spiral tightens around you.

Pain is sometimes the most effective catalyst to get you going. It could be that of a dysfunctional relationship, physical or mental abuse, being stifled, or an agonizing memory. You reach that point where you just can't take any more. Because there's nothing else you can do, you finally relinquish control. You surrender. You let go. You give up.

This could be the most magical turning point of your life. It's the crack that lets in the light.

For you, that fall—that relinquishing of control—signifies utter failure, defeat, death. But not of the things you think. It's the failure of the Ego, that willful child, to control you and your surroundings. It is *its* defeat, *its* death.

Now you have no choice but to look around for a different way to relate to life. You seek solace in a new paradigm, a novel understanding. Is there one? Your circumstances force you into accepting that going with the flow and allowing things to take their own natural course is the only way out at the moment. You also soon begin to realize that nothing is really within your control. And all those "external achievements," no matter how worthy they are, can give you fulfillment only up to a point. Surely no person, or circumstance, should have more power over you than you yourself!

But they do. In fact, your sense of "power," stability, and security stems only from them: a job or a business, the status it gives you, the money you earn and the trappings it provides, the recognition you gain, and the measure of approval you get. Can you trust all of these factors not to let you down again?

Despairing, you agree to look elsewhere for answers. You begin to search for a more secure center of power that won't betray you. Perhaps you begin to read different kinds of books. Maybe you're lucky enough to find a teacher, or a practice that you resonate with. Now you're ready to start a different kind of journey. You'll never be the same again!

☙ ☙ ☙

Chapter 9

EMPOWERMENT: TAKING RESPONSIBILITY FOR YOURSELF

"Freedom is what you do with what's been done to you."

— JEAN-PAUL SARTRE

What is this journey all about?

It's the journey of empowerment, which enables you to become the writer, producer, and director of your own life script. It's the journey that helps you take back the remote-control device for your life. You no longer want others or circumstances to "change channels" at will. From now on, *you* will decide which channels you wish to watch.

It's an inward journey. Why is this so? Why do you need to go within instead of without, where until now you've looked for all the fulfillment you needed? Quite simply, because only *within* can you hope to find an unshakable center of peace. It's where your essential nature, which is made up of joy and love, rests. Everything "without" is changeable. If you're centered in your Self, nothing has the power to shake you.

"The musk is inside the deer, but the deer does not look for it: it wanders around looking for grass."

— Kabir

Did you notice that this Self starts with a capital *S?* Until now, the discussion has centered on the small self—the Ego, the personality, the small mind—that has kept you trapped in a limiting paradigm. The journey of empowerment means that you relate to your world from a strong inner center, the big Self. It's a vast, expansive space that allows Life to happen and you to remain unaffected by it.

Remember the invisible energy layers that surround you? I mentioned the first three in Chapter 1: the physical, mental, and emotional. That's the starting point. You free yourself of aches and pains, you gain mental stability and emotional poise, and then you're ready to move on to relating to your world from "higher" centers—that is, the other layers of your energy body.

Yes, of course, you can choose happiness, peace, and contentment . . . because you've decided that that's how you'll be, *no matter what.* Does that mean that you'll become indifferent to, and remain unmoved by, anything that happens around you? No, as you'll see later in the book, it means that you'll feel even more fully than you do now; you'll be alive to every moment and will live with awareness. You'll choose responses, not let them choose you. You'll learn from your experiences and grow both cognitively and spiritually. Time and time again, you'll learn to select joy and love over pain until it becomes a habit. You'll seek power within, not without.

You can get out of the trap, and you need no one's help. The key is in your possession, and the "trapdoor" opens from the inside.

The first step is taking responsibility for your physical, emotional, and mental well-being. It's like preparing your vehicle for a journey. If it has been taken care of and is in good condition, no matter what the "hurdle," it will effortlessly clear it.

> *"Responsible choice is choosing the harvest before you plant the crop."*
>
> — from *The Mind of the Soul,*
> by Gary Zukav and Linda Francis

Let's start with the physical, the body.

In Chapter 3, I discussed how your body communicates with you and how it's such an accurate gauge for your energy system. In fact, it's like a mirror, reflecting exactly how you're processing life. As I mentioned earlier, the mind is the repository of all kinds of conditioning. Values and beliefs are at the deepest level, at the roots. Beliefs give rise to attitude. From this attitude comes perception, which gives birth to action. As you act, your energy moves in a particular direction. These e-motions make you feel comfortable or uncomfortable. You accept some and reject others. This process, too, if you look closely, is dependent on your beliefs and also on your conditioning.

"Perception: how we see the outside from the inside."

— Anonymous

Every belief of yours is your truth. You may not even recognize it as such, but it's there, deep within you, shaping your responses. Basic beliefs—about life, work, money, family, love, health, and relationships— are implanted by parents, caregivers, teachers, and life circumstances. They get reinforced even as new ones are installed. We live our lives based on these beliefs. Very soon—and one could add, insidiously—they form habitual patterns of relating to others, to circumstances, and to life.

Check out some of these statements. Note which ones you identify with.

- *I am a loser/failure.*

- *Life is unfair.*

- *Fun and happiness are meant for special occasions.*

- *If you laugh too much, you'll cry.*

- *I have no control over my destiny.*

- *To forgive is weakness.*

- *My past was better than my present.*

- *I catch every infection in town.*

- *Health has to deteriorate after 60.*

- *All relationships bring hurt.*

- *Taking time and space for myself is selfish.*

- *People usually let me down.*

- *You can only be successful if you work hard and long.*

- *Rich people are arrogant.*

- *All jobs are stressful.*

- *Being wealthy is for the lucky few!*

Which of these statements have manifested in your life and hold true today? Do you realize that you've helped make them credible?

Like emotions, all beliefs owe their origin to either love/trust or fear/mistrust. Everything that has happened in your life teaches you one or the other. Gradually, one or the other becomes a habitual way of relating.

A fearful mind will be agitated and will blame others and constantly complain—it can't find contentment. It will dwell on regret. It will find fault, be suspicious, and find it hard to trust anybody. The life it shapes will be closed and contracted.

> *"Heavy thoughts bring on physical maladies;*
> *when the soul is oppressed, so is the body."*
>
> — Martin Luther

A quiet, settled mind will be receptive and peaceful. It will take things as they come and understand that each event has a larger purpose. Joyousness and the ability to celebrate, even for no apparent reason, will come easily to it. It will flow with change. The life it molds will be open and expansive.

Which of the two bodies, inhabited by these different minds, would be healthier?

As you begin to understand the body-mind connection, you'll realize that the physical self is only reflecting your responses to life, not its circumstances. An angry, victimized personality will more likely than not simmer in a fire of resentment. It's habituated to revisiting an agonizing incident in all its detail and then diving into the morass of self-pity. No matter how lavish the spread, angry people can neither taste nor digest even a single morsel from the banquet Life offers. The acidity of unforgiveness will regularly rise up in them and finally clog all the arteries of joy. If the mind continues to "mind," the body will reflect these perceived injustices.

An empowered personality will respond to the *same circumstances* differently. The minute you accept that it's your perceptions, worries, guilt, inadequacies, and unprocessed emotions—and not some random external acts—that are causing these telltale aches and pains, you change the equation. Instead of feeling victimized about your dis-ease, and treating pain as a form of "suffering" that has been unfairly meted out to you, you take total responsibility for it. You analyze how you created such pain and then begin to release the bottled-up emotions and heal yourself. It shows you, through your body, what you're unable to see so clearly otherwise. And it offers you the chance to let it go and regain total health.

This process only remains incomplete because you are unaware of this dynamic, refuse to acknowledge it, resist being self-reflective, or are unable to face up to the issues involved or resolve them. In other words, you don't want to "pay the price."

Let's look at this in greater depth. Indigestion of food, as I said in Chapter 3, points to indigestion of something in your life. Greater understanding and acceptance of this "something," be it a person or a circumstance, will immediately lead to relief. Acidity will dissolve if you begin to replace anger with forgiveness. If you lighten your attitude toward a responsibility you might be shouldering, the pain in your shoulders will ease; the knot in your middle back will disappear if you extend compassion to yourself and agree to give up guilt. As the dilemma and fear about a new route you're charting ease, so will the pain in your knees. Release the "waste" that no longer serves you—and you might be surprised that you're no longer constipated! Regain balance in your life and notice as the pain in your ankles dissolves.

"Healing begins with the repair of emotional injuries."

— Caroline Myss

Along with acceptance of others and your life circumstances, turn the lamp of compassion on yourself, too. That's a necessary component of the healing process. After all, what do those emotions that you shun represent? They are parts of yourself that you feel uncomfortable with and don't wish to acknowledge. Jealousy makes you look "bad" in your own eyes. Vulnerability makes you feel weak. Intimacy is scary. Being natural is something you've long forgotten—the real you is deeply hidden behind many preconditioned masks, armors, and defenses.

The process of healing requires that you drop all this "protective gear." You need to accept and love all parts of yourself and stop labeling some dark and others fair. Forgive yourself and begin to feel secure and adequate: That's the price you must pay if you want total healing.

> *"Exploring and embracing our darkness is*
> *the only way we can truly live in the light."*
>
> — Shakti Gawain

To what extent can one stretch this argument? What about terminal illnesses, such as cancer, or other degenerative diseases? The answer is quite simple: You can heal yourself depending on the level of responsibility you're willing to take for having brought about the situation! If you fully accept that, you'll understand that just as you've created it, so do you have the power to heal it fully. Louise Hay, the author of numerous inspirational books that have been translated into all the major languages of the world, is a cancer survivor. She healed herself in a span of six months by setting out on the path of releasing anger, resentment, and self-hatred, which were literally "eating up" her insides.

In my own healing practice, I've witnessed many such miracles: In one instance, kidney stones dissolved because their "owner" came to understand that his bitter nature had formed them; in another, acidity that had been present for two years vanished when the victim realized it represented her anger and feeling of powerlessness and just gave up the negative emotions. In my own case, the aches in my knees evaporated when I was able to recognize the fears that were causing them. I can now sit on the floor cross-legged for eight hours to conduct a workshop; until a few years ago, I found it hard to climb a short flight of stairs. The examples are innumerable. The body-mind connection is irrefutable.

Provided that you're willing to look at the issue causing the physical symptom and resolve or release it, as the case may be, and provided that you're willing to let go of resentment and acrimony and exercise forgiveness, there's nothing you can't heal. And, of course, there's nobody to blame if you can't! Just learn to accurately interpret the results of that laboratory, your body, and you should be able to formulate your own unique healing prescription.

"The 'stuff' that disease is made of requires much more complex treatment than can be given through surgery or drugs alone. It requires, for example, the process of transforming inner grief into lessons that empower rather than destroy the individual."

— from *The Creation of Health,* by C. Norman Shealy, M.D., Ph.D., and Caroline Myss

This is what you owe your body, the vehicle given to you to travel through this lifetime. Listen to it with reverence, and treat it with care. It's always telling you some home truths that can help you heal and grow. For your part, help your body remain healthy and vibrant by constantly clearing out toxic feelings. Even if you think that they're not the *only* causes for ill health, taking responsibility for your physical well-being means accepting that there are at least some emotional components to your dis-ease, which is a symbol of some inner resistance.

Drop it. It's an Ego trap.

☙ ☙ ☙

Chapter 10

DON'T GET TRAPPED
BY YOUR EMOTIONS!

*"We who lived in concentration camps can remember
the men who walked through the huts comforting others,
giving away their last piece of bread. They may have been
few in number, but they offer sufficient proof that everything can be taken from a man but one thing: the last of
the human freedoms—to choose one's attitude in any
given set of circumstances, to choose one's own way."*

— DR. VIKTOR E. FRANKL

What gives Ego traps so much power over us?

Think about any incident that has recently disturbed
you. Feel what happens in your mind and body when
you do. Now think of another harrowing incident that
occurred many years ago. Are you surprised that you can
still cry as you recall the traumatic experience? Why does
the hurt still feel so fresh that it can affect you almost as

much as it did on the day of the event in question? Why can it still re-create the anger, humiliation, shame, guilt, and pain it evoked then?

It's the *quantum* of emotion "locked into" the incident that gives it unrelenting power over you. If this weren't the case, each person would be similarly affected by an identical stimulus.

Consider this scenario: I insult three people. One of them reacts by insulting me back, the second demands an explanation, and the third seems unaffected.

Extend this scenario further: Three weeks later, I ask each of them how they remember the incident. The first is still seething and has decided that he'll neither forgive nor forget. The second has dealt with it, although he still retains some indignation. The third finds it hard to recall what happened! Many years later, the first might have a dysfunctional liver, the second acidity, and the third a healthy body and no emotional residue. Admittedly, this is an exaggerated example, but I hope I've made my point.

It's the emotional component, then, that can keep you *trapped.* Excessive emotions are like a fog, preventing you from seeing clearly. They dictate your responses, which may be inappropriate because, after all, you can't see the whole picture anymore! Fear, disappointment, and regret tie up your energy system in knots. Hurt, worry, doubt, and suspicion literally make holes in this system, through which energy is continually leaked. Anger burns it up. Guilt and depression block its flow. In short, all these emotions *drain* you. They deplete your energy. This, in turn, affects every action, response, and attitude.

Let's take a look again at some of the "energy guzzlers" I discussed earlier (in Chapter 4) in an effort to understand what we can do to "plug" those energy leaks.

> *"The degree of one's emotion varies*
> *inversely with one's knowledge of the facts—*
> *the less you know, the hotter you get."*
>
> — Bertrand Russell

— **Worry** was the first. Have you ever thought of where this often-obsessive feeling stems from? Doesn't it flow from a lack of trust? If so, in whom or what?

Your first answer might be: "In myself." On deeper reflection, you would probably add, "In circumstances going the way I wish them to." If the latter is the case, which it usually is, in *whom*, then, do you lack trust? It's not in yourself, but in a Higher Force. You fear that it won't deliver what you've "requested"!

It's amusing that all chronically worried people to whom I've put the question "Have you ever been supported in the past by something bigger than yourself?" have answered in the affirmative. They've always felt guided and protected, apart from often witnessing or experiencing miracles. Many prayers have been answered. Yet, this time around, they're consumed by worry, because the agony is really "intense."

Too intense for that Higher Power to handle?

Think about it. If you're a worrier, consider whom it is that you're distrusting and doubting.

> *"Faith is the bird that feels the light and*
> *sings when the dawn is still dark."*
>
> — Rabindranath Tagore

You need to understand that you have unnecessarily chained yourself to a wall of fear and anxiety. The moment you begin to regain faith, the shackles will be broken and worry will be banished. More than almost any other emotion, worry is a trap that you can choose not to allow yourself to fall into. It's a habit, and you can break it. I'll talk about how to do so a little later in the chapter.

> *"Love looks forward, hate looks back,*
> *anxiety has eyes all over its head."*

— from *The Neurotic's Notebook,* by Mignon McLaughlin

— Let's take a look at **hurt** and **resentment** now, from an objective distance. Like unwelcome visitors, these drop in without warning, stay long, and are demanding of your time and energy. They're insidious energy pirates: They can leave your coffers empty in just a short while if you allow them.

Remember that analogy about the stones we throw at each other? When do you think you or another person will do that? Will it be on a day when you're feeling wholesome, loving, and good about yourself? No. It will more likely happen when you're feeling low and depleted. Then you'll attempt to "grab" another person's energy. Hurting another, control, manipulation, and domination are some of the easiest ways to do this, especially if your aim is good!

If *you* are the target, just stop and think: Even though the "stone" is personalized—it has to be, otherwise it can't find its mark—does it really "belong" to you? Must you fall into the trap and allow it to wound you? And once it has, how long will you permit yourself to continue bleeding?

The stone isn't yours. It belongs to the person who threw it. Now you have three options: (1) You can receive it but not hurl one back; (2) you can receive it and fling another at the assailant; or (3) you can ignore it, understanding that it's not yours to hold on to. *Whether or not you choose to get hurt—and how much and for how long—depends on you.* Not on anybody else.

If you refuse to let go, then you should realize that you're allowing the person who has hurt you (for whom you may even feel hatred or disgust) to continue to drain you. It's like handing over the code to the locker containing your emotions and allowing him or her to empty it.

"No one can make you feel inferior without your consent."

— Eleanor Roosevelt

Let's start with trying not to fall into the "hurt trap" in the first place. What might make it easier to choose the third option, to not get hurt at all, is to begin understanding that all people do the best they can, at any given point in time. They can only give to others what they are filled with. A rejected person can't make you feel loved. A stressed person will radiate nothing but stress. An angry person can't be compassionate.

Look at some of the people who may have hurt you. Honestly ask yourself, *When they did it, were they really capable of doing anything better?* I'm sure that you'll answer in the negative. And yet, you hold on possessively to the injury caused by that stone—or boulder, as the case may be!

If you really want to be able to handle hurt effectively, just remember: People's treatment of you is more a reflection of their own state than any comment on you!

If you can manage to keep this in mind when something hurtful happens, you'll see the consequences yourself: You won't take it personally. Instead, you'll remind yourself that the other person must have been feeling really depleted while hurling the stone at you! Rather than getting bogged down by your own self-pitying emotions, you can turn your attention to the other individual and try to figure out his or her state of mind. You may think you're doing the person a favor and that it all sounds far too unreal and charitable. Nevertheless, this the best way to not only shield your own energy system from being unnecessarily drained, but also to protect yourself from needless misery.

Try it! With practice, you'll become really good at it. This step might lead to a greater change in your life than anything else in this book! Don't give unreasonable people so much power over you! And practice moving toward tolerance and then compassion instead of toward suffering!

*"Never argue with an idiot! He will take you
down to his level and beat you with experience!"*

— Anonymous

Not taking things personally, however, is one of the most difficult practices! Here's a suggestion that might make it easier: Whenever you get hurt and feel yourself slipping into "darkness," just try to become *aware* of the chatter that's going on in your mind. *How could this have happened to me? How could he [she] have said [done] this to me?* Are these the things that you're constantly asking yourself? If the answer is yes, you know that the issue is becoming very personalized. The last two words of the questions are where your focus is directed: *to me.* Your Ego is getting the better of you.

Now suppose you could just remove these two words. What do the questions read like then? *How could this have happened? How could he [she] have said [done] this?* This changes the focus. Introspect. The process will tell you more about yourself and where you tripped up, besides identifying your emotional triggers and maybe even your emotional patterns. It can also teach you some life lessons.

And just think about it: These are opportunities that you're presented with daily, sometimes in the guise of the smallest, most ordinary incidents. Don't squander them if you can help it! If it doesn't sound too harsh, you should be grateful for those stones and boulders.

And although you must primarily use these opportunities for self-reflection, you may still need to communicate and express yourself to the other person in the relationship. Do so, but not in the midst of a heated argument. Later on, tell him or her exactly how you feel. If you really want the other person to listen and appreciate your viewpoint, start your sentences with "I felt hurt when . . ." rather than "You hurt me with . . ." When you're blaming others or your circumstances, or complaining (especially in a whining tone), people's natural instinct is to shut down the auditory faculty in order to protect themselves. They can't hear you because they're busy preparing their defenses.

In such a situation, you feel more misunderstood and more hurt. It might help to remember that both people—yes, that means *you,* too—are actually closed to listening when the most important thing is to be proved right. It's like talking to another person with your iPod headphones jammed in your ears. You want to listen only to your "chosen song"—that is, your argument. The other person does the same. Your shouts grow louder and louder. But can either of you hear? No . . . nor are you ready to.

It's not easy, but someone needs to stop playing the "hurt game," which requires a minimum of two players! If you stop buying into it, your partner can't play. Refuse to be hooked by guilt, pity, or false "niceness." Try not to adulterate the hurt with the past or future.

We often reinforce an injury or slight by reminding ourselves of its history, thus enlarging it. We also start believing in generalizations, presuming things that are usually not true.

Ponder this: When someone says or does something hurtful, have you ever wondered why the statement or deed has so much power? After all, it's only an individual's opinion; why isn't it easy to disregard? Perhaps because it contains a seed of truth that you resonate with?

If I told you that you have horns on your head, you'd find it easy to laugh and dismiss my comment. But if I were to tell you that you're irresponsible, lazy, or clumsy—and if you believed my words—you'd be offended. I would only be mirroring what you feel about yourself, as do all the people around you—especially those close to you—who show you just what you needed to see, helping you on your journey of growth and self-discovery. The ones who irritate and upset you the most are your greatest teachers. Through their actions, words, and responses, they're helping you learn the lesson you most need to, even if they're bringing out the worst in you! The worst resides *in you*. The other person is just a trigger.

— The worst in you includes **jealousy.** The arrow of this emotion penetrates deeply and quickly. And it's very hard to extricate. While it's embedded within you, it saps your energy. As you continue to get depleted, you lash out at others, uncontrollably and often viciously. But it's like fighting demons in the dark. Since jealousy is one of the most difficult emotions to honestly admit to, especially to yourself, you become increasingly manipulative, scheming, and possessive as you seek to camouflage it under other feelings and blame others to regain control.

Don't attempt to seek control outside. The only solution is to take a hard look within and get rid of the self-doubt and insecurity that are driving you in the wrong direction—toward darkness.

— If you don't take remedial measures soon, you'll find it hard to get out of this darkness and start wallowing in the well of **self-pity.** People in this state aren't good company. They drain others as they seek to suck energy that they themselves lack. If you're planning to take responsibility for yourself, jumping out of this well would be a great "muscle" toner and one of the first "exercises" you need to perform!

So, getting hurt offers a huge potential for growth. It reveals to you what you need to see, it shows you the areas you need to work on, and it gives you the opportunity to expand your limits of tolerance and acceptance. Reduced to one sentence, *growth is about choosing an expanded paradigm over a contracted one.* So instead of channeling your energy into feeling offended and resentful, grab the chance to shift gears and change habitual patterns that no longer serve you.

How do you achieve this objective? Is there any technique that that can stop your energy from being drained and prevent people and circumstances from "stealing" your power? There's only one way—it's not easy, but perhaps it becomes more feasible when you figure out that it benefits you more than the others. It is *forgiveness*.

Consider what unforgiveness does. It keeps every wound open even as it closes the heart. And who else bleeds but the person who can't forgive? Akin to a cancer that corrodes your various bodily systems or a termite that eats away covertly at a piece of wood, the feeling leaves you hollow, empty, and ready to crumble at a touch. It drains you physically, mentally, and emotionally. Unforgiveness is a full stop, a conclusion: It's a choice you've made that imprisons you.

Why, then, do you hold on to this feeling so tenaciously? Because this is where your Ego steps in, reminding you that you would be considered weak, foolish, vulnerable, and somehow guilty if you forgave. The Ego dictates that the other person doesn't deserve your pardon. It's very important for you to be proven "right." Haven't you noticed the pride and the sense of power, bordering on arrogance, in people's voices when they declare that they'll never forgive?

There needn't be a full stop. Forgiveness is a comma in the middle of the sentence that permits healing, growth, and enlightenment. It's a sign of emotional poise and maturity. It's for the strong, not for the weak, releasing energy that can be used beneficially for other activities. It's immensely freeing . . . it's the best gift you can give yourself.

"Always forgive your enemies;
nothing annoys them so much."

— Oscar Wilde

And when you're ready to forgive, you can choose to offer an even more potent soul tonic: compassion. To "administer" this healing potion to another person, you need to really reach out of yourself, ignore the Ego and its demands, set aside your own ideas of who and what is right and wrong, and go ahead and proffer uncon- ditional love. The tonic works even better (for you!) if you think the other person doesn't "deserve" it. And yet, those who merit it the least need it the most. When you can offer it even to them, the return gift of expan- sion, healing, and growth that you'll be giving yourself is invaluable.

"Forgiveness is letting go of all hopes for a better past."

— Gerald G. Jampolsky, M.D.

— Of course, you can't hope to forgive another human being if you haven't extended that favor to yourself. If you're still carrying the burden of **guilt** and **regret,** you can't hope to look life straight in the eye, experience joy, and walk with a lightness in your step. If you accept that people indeed do the best they can at a certain point in time, given their energy resources and other constraints they're facing, then apply the same rule to yourself.

Guilt and regret are a couple of the heaviest and dens- est emotions, blocking all points of energy entry. You need to put that heavy burden down. Carrying it won't change the past. Constant punishment rarely does. And beware! This is one of the easiest devices others use to steal your energy.

— You must also protect yourself against **fear**, another greedy energy thief. It enters very easily where doubt, worry, and distrust have left the doors unlocked. Together the gang manages to blindfold and lock faith and its ally, trust, in the cellar. Now they can smash and grab—until you, the house's owner, realize what's really happening and unleash the guards. But you may be too late. In a very short while—because this notorious gang has perfected its act—you can be left emotionally bankrupt.

Why do we find it so hard to confront these marauders? We neither raise an alarm nor put up a fight, until it's too late. When we're in their grip, we feel terrorized and immobilized, as if in a hypnotic state. We tend to forget that fear is in fact a bully and, like most bullies, a coward, too. If we were able to face fear squarely, we would see it slinking away.

Do just that the next time something frightens you. It's an imaginary reality. If you can, tackle it head-on. Think of the worst that would happen if the scenario you're imagining really occurred. Dissect it. You might be surprised to find that you have all the necessary resources to cope with the situation. Use a healing modality (if you know one) to release fear. (You'll take up a few such modalities later in these pages.) Think of some of the tough times in your life and how you handled them. You seemed to have superhuman strength—you need to convince yourself that you still do. Don't lose faith.

"Character isn't inherited. One builds it daily
by the way one thinks and acts, thought by thought,
action by action. If one lets fear or hate or anger take
possession of the mind, they become self-forged chains."

— Helen G. Douglas

— **Anger** is another web, spun by the Ego, to entrap you. It stems from a feeling of being out of control. If somebody opposes you vehemently or you feel thwarted in some way, you lose your cool. Yet, have you thought about what lies beneath the dark cloak of rage? It's usually a fearful, insecure little boy or girl, who has decided that the only way to be heard is to be loud and aggressive. In actuality, anger is a defense mechanism that you choose to protect yourself from being hurt again. By being hostile, you can keep people away; protect your "turf"; and keep yourself from falling back into a vulnerable, soft space of love. It's a fine way of deflecting energy from the real job of looking within and healing the hurt and pain—an excuse to not do "homework."

And if you're the kind of person who allows others to terrorize you with loud words, violence, or crossness, you're not doing them any favors. You're only pushing them into a morass of guilt, low self-esteem, and denial. Stop being terrorized. Just as you wouldn't offer an alcoholic another glass of liquor, don't allow an angry person to continually get away with loud-voiced domination. Anger is a sickness, and angry people need help.

"Holding on to anger is like grasping
a hot coal with the intent of throwing it at
someone else; you are the one who gets burned."

— the Buddha

97

Well, you might be thinking—and rightly so—that this is all "feel-good" advice, but wouldn't it be quite "unhuman" not to ever get hurt or jealous or angry or worried? I agree. All emotions are sanctioned. But holding on to them endlessly isn't the way of the enlightened. Stuck records are jarring.

"Love is a choice you make from moment to moment."

— Barbara De Angelis

As you begin to grow in emotional maturity and to see e-motions (especially the negative ones) for what they are—movements of energy, gauges of your energy system—and as you begin to accept that you're responsible for giving them power over you, slowly but surely you'll work your way out of their grip and walk more freely than you ever did. You'll also come to recognize the enticements of the Ego and be able to reject them. Each time you do that, the voice of the Higher Self will be heard louder and more clearly, and you'll be able to begin plugging the "energy leaks."

In practical terms, what can you do on a daily basis, starting this minute, every time you get hurt, worried, fearful, suspicious, doubtful, and angry? Here are a few suggestions:

- Become watchful and start recognizing your e-motions. What do they point to within you?

- Instead of "owning" draining emotions, choose to drop them. Constantly practice putting them "in the fire" (see Chapter 12).

If you can't do that, take the easy way out:
Feel them fully and release them (see
Chapter 13).

- Stop playing the "hurt game."

- Learn to recognize the Ego and when it's
  attempting to dominate you. Each time, try
  to choose a Higher Self–directed response.

- As soon as you can, step back and attempt to
  see the Bigger Picture. Change the "zoom"
  (Ego) lens for the "panoramic" (Higher Self)
  one! (See Chapter 15.)

- At the same time, recognize the people
  who "torment" you as your most valuable
  teachers.

- Remember to cut cords (see Chapter 16)
  to keep your energy system clear and
  uncluttered.

Doing all these things will move you to a space of
gratitude and enable you to access the most efficacious
remedy: forgiveness.

Think of the entire process as a weight-loss program.
You're going to change your emotional diet, switching
over from eating junk to healthy, empowering foods.

Sweet, carbonated drinks of hurt, with no redeeming
qualities at all, are banned.

Calorie-rich foods of hate and blame aren't allowed.
And if you occasionally do go out and binge, you balance and detoxify yourself as soon as you can.

You refuse to stuff yourself with the creamy pastry of self-pity.

You exercise your muscles of self-awareness and slowly develop tone and fitness.

You begin to understand deeply the consequences of your indulgences and deviations.

Will the process be easy? Maybe not. Temptations to slip back into past patterns will entice you. You'll feel frustrated and low at regular intervals. Often the scale will tell you that you haven't lost a single ounce. It will all seem worthless and ineffective. At times, you'll even feel disconcerted as you sense old patterns breaking and you don't really recognize this new you, who feels unfamiliar and strange. This new "freedom" could be frightening. But if you persevere, you'll begin to reap rewards.

With the passage of time, you'll start to feel good about yourself. Your stamina and energy levels will improve. You'll come to feel in charge. As the "flab" of limiting beliefs starts diminishing, you'll begin to experiment with new styles of dressing, new getups, and new relationships. Much to your surprise, each one will suit you. It will be a makeover! You'll begin doing things you could never have dreamed of. The compliments from those around you will fuel your motivation. Finally, you'll push yourself right out of the energy-sapping trap you'd fallen into.

※ ※ ※

Chapter 11

THE MIND: FROM CONTROL TO FLOW

"The 'No!' mind is agitated, doubting and miserable. The 'Yes!' mind is quiet, holistic and joyful. 'Yes!' is an acknowledgment of knowledge."

— SRI SRI RAVI SHANKAR

The key to getting out of the trap is the cultivation of a restful and tranquil mind!

It's quite clear now that much of our stress is caused by the activity of the mind, whose interpretation of situations is what creates havoc. It's also equally clear that long after an event is actually over, it can keep on replaying in our heads, like a horror movie that never ends. A restless mind constantly flirts with the past and the future. Unknowingly, it "cheats on" the present moment, thereby losing the most valuable gift it has.

Painful situations surface in everybody's life, but suffering needn't be the response. The first reaction is an external circumstance that's out of your control. However, the second is an internal one, which you can completely modulate! And that depends on how well rested and tranquil your mind is.

A well-rested mind is very efficient because it works smart, not hard! It does its job when it needs to, and after that it rests. It doesn't have to prove its worth by constantly doing something, so it takes breaks whenever it's not busy. Is it a slacker or lazy? Is its inactivity a sign of dullness? No, quite the opposite: Because this mind is relaxed and not feverish, it's focused, alert, and very creative. It's receptive to new ideas. It doesn't like to waste energy in trying to dominate the situation or dictate terms to others. It enjoys the flow of events and accepts them as they are. A smart mind is a quiet mind. It's an asset, not a hindrance.

What do you think is the quality of *your* mind? Is it busy? Is it still? Is it ruffled? Is it restless? Is it judgmental? Is it accepting? And most important, do *you* control it, or vice versa? Can you imagine the quality of your life if you have a negative, restless, and agitated mind? Or a volatile, volcanic one? On the other hand, imagine if it were more like a serene, sparkling lake. More than anything else, it's the quality of your mind and how much it controls you that determines the quality of your life.

Here's an interesting exercise: Just stop reading for a moment and check how many breaths you're taking per minute. (One inhalation and one exhalation count as a single breath.) Make them normal ones, not attempting to lengthen or shorten them. When you take 18 breaths per minute, you have 120 thoughts per second. If you take 12 a minute, this number falls to 20.

From time immemorial, two of the most crucial functions of the breath have been to support you and come to your aid whenever necessary. When you face danger (read: *stress*), it quickens and becomes shallow to supply you with the oxygen you need to "fight" or "flee" from the calamity. When the crisis has passed, the breath slows down.

In our stressed, rushed lives today, our *normal* breath is fast and shallow! It never slows down.

The number of breaths you're taking per minute is a good indicator of your level of stress. The optimum is 11 to 12. If you're breathing faster, and most of us are, your mind is cluttered with too many thoughts. That's why when you're stressed, you feel confused and unclear. You're unable to "think straight." It's the same when you're angry. You remain on high alert, and so does your mind. High brain activity isn't synonymous with clarity. You'll never make right decisions in such a state.

> *"Life is in the breath*
> *therefore he who half breathes, half lives."*

— from *The Healing Handbook,* by Tara Ward

What can you do to cultivate a smart, sparkling mind if you haven't already done so? You can take the most logical action.

What would you do if you needed to de-stress, if you were really exhausted and had to refresh yourself, or if you'd been working too hard and tirelessly? You would take a break; you would stop the tiring activity for a while. You would switch off your "mobile" mind. If its battery was low, you would recharge it.

How do you tell your mind to just shut down? When you try to do so, you run into a number of "technical" problems: It doesn't know how to. It doesn't listen to you. And it doesn't want to, because it would then have to relinquish control, and that's frightening. Do you have any access to your mind at all?

You may have got a clue from the exercise referred to earlier in this chapter. The simplest doorway to enter the mind is the breath. Like the steering wheel of a vehicle, it's the only way you have of guiding the movement of the mind.

Stop reading for a few minutes and do the exercise in the next paragraph. Observe how you feel. You might even want to bring up a disturbing emotion, go through the steps, and then check how you feel about it.

> *Just start observing your breath. Concentrate totally on its inflow . . . the coolness as it enters your nostrils. Follow it down your spine and then back up out the top of your head. Continue to do so for a few minutes. Keep focused on it. You'll be surprised to realize that while you're noticing your breath, you have no thoughts. They might interrupt, but if you take your attention back to the breath, they're banished. Your mind can do only one thing at a time!*

Think about it: What a wonderful resource you have at your disposal to instantly calm the mind! You can do it anyplace, anytime, and you don't need any fancy tools or gadgets for it other than *awareness*.

Breath control is one quick method of calming yourself in the most stressful situations. It helps you take a much-needed pause to choose your response instead of repeating what you've habitually been doing. That's the reason behind the advice to breathe ten times before saying or doing anything when you're angry. I'm sure you can appreciate the potential to extend it further. If this method can bring you peace under pressure in a few minutes, why not do it for a longer time when you already *are* peaceful? Maybe you'll never come to feel so "pressurized."

The fact is, this rest is just what the mind needs to keep itself cool. At the moment it's like a heated engine that has been running ceaselessly. If you want to extend the life of that engine so it keeps serving you all life long, allow it to rest regularly. The method you may be adopting now could be more akin to opening the hood and throwing cold water on the engine because it's already steaming and is about to blow up! Instead, you might consider giving your mind a break so that you never reach such a crisis.

Just sit and do nothing for at least ten minutes per day. Watch what happens. Slowly, little by little, the restlessness will begin to ease. The tight muscles will relearn what it means to relax. Instead of finding those ten minutes endless, as you might on the first day, soon you'll begin to look forward to that "vacation." Gradually, you can extend the time of peace that you so richly deserve.

The long-term benefits are amazing. To your surprise, you discover that this stillness begins to permeate your day. Your capacity to cope grows. You find yourself alert and active. You're increasingly more responsive and less reactive. Thoughts slow down . . . and as they do, you're able to find the "gaps" that allow you to choose wiser responses. Slowly, you begin to "train" your mind rather than letting it run amok.

The mind is naturally inclined to dwell on the negative. And you encourage it! Often, you seek lots of information from it. Like search engines on the Internet, it displays all the related links for you. Do you realize that what the mind finds depends totally on the instructions that you feed it? Try altering them and observe the new results. The very quality of your thoughts will begin to change. Your "positive vibrations" will shift to a higher frequency.

As the mind begins to understand that the fear and alienation it had been taught to guard against are not as real as it believed, it allows Love to get its stifled voice back. The heart begins to be heard once more. It sings of connectivity, belongingness, and oneness. The mind learns that there's no cause to distrust it.

And so the mind and heart start to work together, in a fine balance, supporting one another and collaborating —instead of competing—with each other. The journey of growth gives the heart its rightful place back. The mind and heart start to learn from and even appreciate each other. Instead of seeing everything as black and white—defined and set—you begin to see other colors as well. Life becomes so much more enjoyable! Judgments diminish, the Ego quiets down, and your world expands. The sense of curiosity and adventure, which had been shut out until now, flows back in. You begin to experience joy and well-being spontaneously, unconnected to any reason.

One day, you realize that uncertainty doesn't frighten you as much as it once did. You don't need to control everything around you to feel stable. You allow Life to "happen" in its own way and feel perfectly equipped to cope with it.

Slowly, the resistance that you've held on to so tightly begins to melt, and the physical aches and pains that have been trapped in your body are released—and you're relieved to see them leave! The hardened emotions that were the cause soften and dissolve. And you don't hold on to the *new* aches and pains as they arise. Your energy system clears up and remains free of clutter.

You begin to live in a state of flow rather than resistance. My friend Rupa Israel described this development aptly when she summed up a vacation she'd just spent with her daughter as "just General Joy and Total Love." That is flow: surrender to, and acceptance of, what is. "Be in GJ and TL no matter what!" is our reminder to each other!

Chapter 12

AWARENESS: EXERCISING AN INTROSPECTIVE CHOICE

"Sometimes your joy is the source of your smile, but sometimes your smile can be the source of your joy."

— THICH NHAT HANH

Living vibrantly and joyously—being in GJ and TL—is our essential nature. This is how we're meant to live. Unfortunately, we've forgotten how to do so! To get back to where we started from, we have to unlearn some limiting habits and attitudes.

In order for this to happen, we have to begin to live more consciously and with awareness.

At first it's akin to turning on all the lights in a cluttered room. Now you know exactly what you have to do! You have to clear it up to make it more habitable—this is the first choice you need to make. Do you want to do so . . . or are you content to merely take a look, turn the lights off, and pretend you never saw the mess at all?

> *"Every choice you make brings a possible future into your reality."*
>
> — from *The Mind of the Soul,* by Gary Zukav and Linda Francis

If you've read this book up to this point, it's safe to assume that you didn't pick the second option! Awareness means exercising an introspective choice. Given the understanding you have of the interaction between the mind, body, and emotions, and given your intention to live more fully and joyfully, you're now going to choose your responses moment by moment. At present, you may be reacting to situations in a knee-jerk fashion: An action triggers an automatic *re*action. People who are aware are able to make a small pause between the two and decide what their response should be.

> *"Awakening is a shift in consciousness in which thinking and awareness separate."*
>
> — from *A New Earth,* by Eckhart Tolle

Instead of allowing your mind, thoughts, and emotions to manipulate you like a puppet on a string, you can choose which you wish to entertain. You may not immediately be able to choose your visitors. You never know who's ringing the doorbell, but you *can* decide whether or not you want to let the person in and how much time you wish to spend with him or her. You may decide to just look through the keyhole and not open the door at all, especially when you know that your visitor is a drain on your energy. You've met before—if permitted entry, he or she settles down and shows no signs of leaving. Some visitors are clever, though. They sneak in through the back door. You wouldn't choose to offer a thief the best chair in your living room, would you?

When you make a habit of deciding which kinds of thoughts and emotions you want for company, you've already accepted an amazing truth. You can look at them and decide so you know that *you* are neither those thoughts nor those emotions. You are much more than that. They are, at best, visitors. And you henceforth treat them as such. You make your own boundaries based on what's best for you! You cultivate close friendships with the ones that make you feel good and you refuse to associate with those that don't.

> *"The closest to being in control we will ever be is in that moment when we realize we're not."*
>
> — Brian Kessler

In the following paragraph is a process that offers a really easy way of becoming aware of what goes on in your mind! This is a beautiful little trick I learned from Sally Perry, a Native American healer. Don't fight or judge the thoughts. Just become aware of them and do what you need to: "burn" them and return to your essential Higher Self. (You can do it with emotions, too.)

> *Visualize a purple fire burning near you. You can "light" it anytime you like and keep it lit the whole day. It moves with you. Every time you think a "negative" thought, catch it, say "in the fire," and drop it there. Watch it burn. Replace it with a happy thought. Do the same with bothersome emotions.*

You'll be amazed by how many times you'll be saying "in the fire" in the first few days you start this exercise.

Similarly, you become more familiar with the Ego and its need to control you. You treat it with compassionate firmness. As you continue to do that, it understands its place and increasingly begins to serve you. It provides you with the healthy sense of self that you need, but it doesn't seek to alienate you. If it forgets and attempts to manipulate you into habitual patterns, you don't fall for the bait. And if by chance you do, at least you know that this time you got "hooked," and you do what you need to do to *un*hook yourself. Just like salt in food, you need just the right amount of Ego to make things tasty and palatable. Now you can align it to serve you and your life purpose instead of the other way around, as it was before.

Remember, though, that awareness is a soft-focus bulb, not a harsh floodlight. Don't practice it so stringently that you forget to live. The aim isn't to be judgmental of yourself as you continue to grow, but to gently guide yourself out of the maze of limiting habits and conditioning. Don't castigate yourself when you slip or fall. Dust yourself off, learn from the experience, and move on. Become aware that each "troublesome" situation is a gift, because it allows you to choose either the habitual "trapping" pattern or a new "empowering" one. You can choose to either expand or contract—the more you expand, the freer you become. The ultimate aim of growth is to respond from a vast space of Love in every situation. And that process starts with *you*.

❀ ❀ ❀

Chapter 13

FEELING
FULLY AGAIN

*"If we could see the miracle of a single flower
clearly, our whole life would change."*

— THE BUDDHA

Awareness—which is another way of saying that
you're relating to events and situations from a higher
consciousness—also gives you a wiser and kinder understanding of the Ego, your mind, and your emotions.
In fact, they're your guides on this journey of life. If it
weren't for the Ego, how would you know what your
limits are, which areas need your attention, and which
particular "traps" you routinely fall into? It's the Ego,
then, that "sets up" your lessons for the day, and how
well you learn them is the gauge.

And it's your emotions, allied with the Ego, that
guide you to your vulnerable spaces. We all have a "pain-

body," as Eckhart Tolle describes it. The easiest access to it is through these spaces, and as you begin to connect with them, you'll be clearing out long-held "waste." You'll understand that you don't need to resist, fight, or judge your emotions. Just allow them to flow.

Harish Nirula, a beloved teacher, taught me this most profound practice. In actuality, it's more than that—it's a way of living. What it seeks to do is to take us back to doing what we all once did naturally but have forgotten: being childlike. In Chapter 2, I spoke about how conditioning erodes naturalness, simplicity, and honesty. This way of being dissolves such conditioning more easily and permanently than any intellectual understanding. As a first step of aware, conscious living, then, you begin to recognize emotions and thoughts and choose states of being.

First of all, it means beginning to feel fully again. In an effort to be in control and appear mature, we've tried to repress, suppress, and hide hurt and pain, often refusing to acknowledge them even to ourselves. Thinking positive and being in control are new mantras that have suffocated spontaneity. We've become dishonest with ourselves. Authenticity has vanished. Masks shield us from developing intimacy in relationships.

"Ignorance of your emotions results in your being controlled
by parts of yourself that are generating your emotions."

— from *The Heart of the Soul,*
by Gary Zukav and Linda Francis

The first step to reclaiming that essence of our being is becoming childlike in the way we process emotions. Gently allow yourself to open up to experiencing all of them—the good, the bad, and the ugly. In fact, stop labeling them as such. Accept that some emotions are comfortable and others not. In spite of that, don't banish either variety. If possible, be more loving toward those that upset you. Allow them to tell you what they need. I described them earlier as "naughty children"; treat them as exactly that. Neither judge nor indulge them.

When you become proficient at this, do you realize what you're actually doing? You are, in fact, detaching yourself from the emotion and looking at it. Just this "looking" has the power to dissolve most of your misery about the situation. Try it!

And once you've let the feeling fully express itself, neither dwell nor wallow in it. Bless it and allow it to leave. That, in fact, is what it's trying to do as it draws your attention. If you don't imprison it, if you don't attach a possessive "mine" to it, and if you don't clutch on to it, it will float right out of you, leaving your energy system clean and clear and you feeling peaceful and calm. The less you resist emotions, the less their power to irritate or provoke you. In fact, as you continue to acknowledge and release them, you'll realize that far from being irritants, these movements of energy are doorways to enlightenment.

This is how you do it: Become observant with respect to your body, one of your most valuable teachers. When you feel emotional about something, turn all your attention toward your physical being. Just monitor the sensations you're experiencing and where in your body they occur. You might feel tightness in one part; heaviness in another; and tingling, choking, churning, or discomfort elsewhere. Now just *be* totally with this bodily sensation *instead of* indulging your mind and allowing it to lead you astray. This "instead of" is the crux of this process. *You must get <u>out of</u> your mind and stop thinking for a while and get <u>into</u> your body and begin feeling the different sensations.*

Performing this activity takes some practice. The feeling you're trying to pinpoint might intensify for a few minutes or turn into something else. Continue to give it your loving attention, with full awareness. Most important, consciously breathe into it. Attempt to inhale and exhale slowly and deeply.

Do you realize that when you face "danger," stress, or an unpleasant situation, you actually stop breathing or else take shallow "half-breaths." You do so because you're resisting the feeling, pushing it away, and denying it. As it settles into your body as an "energy knot" and later as a physical pain, it becomes something to fear, something to be dreaded.

Now, as you begin to practice conscious nonjudgmental breathing, these stuck feelings actually dissolve and you experience a rare restfulness. They won't bother you again. You'll neither hold on to them nor need to regurgitate them. They will be gone.

> *"Emotion in itself is not unhappiness. Only emotion plus an unhappy story is unhappiness."*
>
> — from *A New Earth,* by Eckhart Tolle

The secret is to give up making judgments: *Why am I feeling like this? I shouldn't be feeling like that. Why did I lose my temper again? Why am I not able to get out of the well of self-pity? Why do I still feel regret or hurt or disappointment?* If you strive to accept what is, exactly as it is without subjecting it to judgmental dissection, you'll begin to flow with whatever is happening. Think about it: Isn't this an easier way to "be" than what you're presently doing? Right now you feel emotions, which may in themselves be uncomfortable. Additionally, you tend to fight them!

If, instead of resisting, you now develop a friendship with emotions and accept them, they, in turn, express themselves and prepare to leave, taking with them others in the same category. You then begin to feel more whole in body, mind, and spirit. You also begin to feel an unusual sense of tranquility. The same emotions that trapped you will now become your doorway to freedom.

Once again—although this time with awareness—you'll start to live as you did when you were a child: innocent, natural, carefree, and spontaneous. You won't be afraid to be yourself. You'll be in unconditional love: with yourself and then with Life and all it offers.

In children, these qualities are inborn. Kids really don't know any better! In an aware adult who lives like this, they're a sign of ultimate growth.

You, too, can be that childlike adult. And with the guilelessness of a child, who doesn't understand parental constraints, you must ask of the Universe all you desire and trust that it will give it to you.

Chapter 14

INTENDING,
MANIFESTING,
RECEIVING

*"The universe holds its breath as we choose, instant by instant,
which pathway to follow; for the universe, the very essence of
life itself, is highly conscious. Every act, thought, and choice
adds to a permanent mosaic; our decisions ripple through the
universe of consciousness to affect the lives of all."*

— FROM *POWER vs. FORCE,*
BY DAVID R. HAWKINS, M.D., Ph.D.

Living with awareness has unexpected bonuses!
Now that the mind is freer, it can begin to do something
more adventurous and magical! Not involved with only
control and contraction now, the "small mind" expands
to connect with the Big Mind, the place of infinite pos-
sibility and potential. The understanding dawns that we
can set actions in motion with intent. Feverish activity is
replaced by effortless faith in a Higher Force that each of

us is connected with. Thoughts are our messengers. So as we begin to monitor and choose them, now with awareness, exactly what we desire begins to manifest. This is how it all happens.

In Chapter 9, I discussed the power of beliefs. Our faith in them—our acceptance of them as truth—actually creates them! Where do they reside? In the subconscious mind . . . which, by the way, isn't just a part of your brain, as you might imagine. It actually exists in every cell; each has an innate intelligence, memory, and belief system, if we could call it that.

So to delve deeper, what *is* a belief? It's a thought—not just an ordinary thought, though. It's one that has an emotional charge to it. It possesses an intensity of feeling, which in fact gives it its power. It's firmly rooted because of that power. It has grown strong because it has been repeated and reinforced hundreds of times . . . or, sometimes, implanted by the intensity, the shock, or even the trauma of the moment.

For example, you may have repeatedly heard statements such as these when you were growing up: "You're so clumsy," "Your time management is poor," "You look so lovely in whatever you wear," or "You'll always do well in life." These first "impressions" of you actually *become* you! You begin to "live" them because they were expressed at a point when you were young, vulnerable, and unquestioning of their accuracy. Gradually, as you continued to believe in them, they did become your living reality. If you identified with some of the belief statements in Chapter 9, you saw how true you are to them!

Sometimes early beliefs get shaken and even replaced by other, more commanding ones. For example, you may come from a generally trusting space but get involved in a relationship that breaks your heart. A new belief about relationships will now be planted in you. If it takes strong root, it will continue to shape your reality. Now you'll actually begin to attract more such interactions that leave you feeling let down. Traumas, accidents, and sudden shocks can also give rise to certain mini-truths.

So a belief, then, is an idea—a frozen thought that, for various reasons, has the power and sanction of being, at least for you, the truth. *Your* truth. Near undeniable.

Now, let's see how thoughts function. They're live entities, and energy follows them. So if you're worrying, for example, about the poor health of a relative, about whether or not your child will get into a good university, about your new business venture, or about your financial security, you're actually sending energy to those thoughts. Worry implies that the thoughts aren't happy ones. So, all the time that you sit and think them, you're *actually* channeling energy to *actually* making that which you fear happen. The same applies to fears that you might focus on or feelings of inadequacy, victimization, and hopelessness. That is the immense power thoughts contain—each little dart that you send out into the Universe embodies an intention of what you want.

It may not be *exactly* what you want, but the Universe, waiting there to grant it to you, doesn't know that. It's totally nonjudgmental, and generous, ready to do your bidding: to give you exactly what you're focusing on, to expand it in your life. There's no dearth in its coffers, and what you ask for doesn't take away from anyone else's share. If you ask with fervor, with feeling, and with intensity, the Universe gets the message and your request is sanctioned. That's how easy it is. That's how powerful *you* are. That's how you have, in fact, until this moment created your reality.

Look around you: at your life, the state of your relationships, and the circumstances you find yourself in. You've created each of them. Now, you might question this. *If only* wishes were fulfilled so easily, then there should be no poverty, no disease, no violence, and no terrorism or other mishaps in the world. But all these are "needed" as well. In fact, they, too, are differing experiences and setups chosen by souls in the process of evolution. (I'll talk more about this in the next chapter.)

As you decide to take full responsibility for yourself and live with awareness, you'll begin to understand the real meaning of not needing to blame anyone for the space you find yourself in. With a sense of awe, you'll realize that if you could summon that which you didn't want, then by changing a belief or a thought, you can replace it with something new and desired. And all you need to do is begin watching your thoughts. Be careful about the messages you're sending to the Universe. And become vigilant about the ones you're receiving.

The time we usually ask the Universe, God, or a Higher Power to grant our desires is when we pray. We sit with eyes closed, head bowed, and hands folded and make an appeal for whatever is missing in our lives. We speak aloud our worries and fears and ask that we be absolved of them. We pray for abundance in certain areas. Sometimes we offer bribes in the form of pilgrimages, donations, and the like.

All that would be fine, though, if we just retained the fervor and faith that we manifest during prayer time. The problem arises because the moment we get up from it, we negate it all by reinforcing that troublesome thought, that doubt, and that lack of faith that tell us the wish won't be granted. Unfortunately, that fearful voice has a stronger power than the one that prayed.

It's more frequent and persistent. And so it wins. We're creating a reality, although with lack of awareness.

"All the powers in the universe are already ours. It is we who have put our hands before our eyes and cry that it is dark."

— Swami Vivekananda

Every thought is akin to a request to the Universe. Depending on how clear the intention behind each thought is, it is manifest: the clearer the intent, and the stronger the faith in its occurrence, the quicker the manifestation. Can you imagine how many such thoughts we waste, misuse, or remain blissfully unaware of?

"If you manage to stay purely focused upon any thought for as little as 68 seconds, the vibration is powerful enough that its manifestation begins."

— from *Ask and It Is Given,* by Esther and Jerry Hicks

Make a list of all the circumstances, relationships, and facets of your life that give you joy. Then make a list of those that <u>don't.</u> See if you can find a belief about those things lurking within. Start to change it, using positive affirmations, awareness, and introspection.

Now let's begin to make new intentions:

- Name one thing that you would really like to manifest in your life. Be as specific as possible. Describe it in great detail—with dates, times, and amounts, as the case may be.

- Close your eyes, sit in a comfortable position, and take a few deep breaths right up to your navel. Tell your body to relax and remain still. Instruct your mind to be calm. Touch your first finger to your thumb, making a circle.

- Now visualize the circumstance occurring. Inject colors, sounds, and flavors into your picture. Feel all the emotions connected with the happy moment as strongly as possible. Declare loudly, three times, that it has already manifested. For example: "X is well, healthy, and out of the hospital," "Y has been admitted to Harvard," or "My business is booming."

- Feel gratitude for having received the gift of your wish manifesting. This step is extremely important. Gratitude raises your vibratory level, making you open to receiving.

- Now leave it to the Universe, the Higher Force that you trust, to take care of your desire. This is as important as all the earlier steps. Just as you wouldn't keep breathing down your assistant's neck after you've given him or her a task to do, let the Universe accomplish *its* job.

- When you feel ready, take another few deep breaths and open your eyes.

Repeat the visualization exercise with total faith as often as you wish but at least once daily.

This is a four-step process:

1. You ask with faith.

2. You don't pollute it with doubt or mistrust. You let the "seed" take root in well-nourished soil. Doubt sends mixed messages to the Universe.

3. Rather than wasting energy figuring out how it's going to happen, you concentrate on getting yourself ready to receive.

4. Once your intent manifests, you acknowledge it and remember to express gratitude.

All the steps are supported by energy laws. First, whatever you focus on expands. It is the "placing of the order." Second, provided that you don't keep changing your mind about it, production commences. Third, there's never any doubt that the production takes place; delivery, however, is often impeded because when the doorbell rings, you don't open the door. In energetic terms, you can only receive at the same "vibratory" level as the one you're at. This takes some doing. (A few simple ideas for achieving this are presented later on in the book.) Fourth, giving gratitude helps you stay at a level that encourages still more manifestation.

This lovely little process is profound and effective. Now you're not only choosing states of being but also actually co-creating the circumstances of your life. Affirm everything with a childlike faith, yet open yourself to welcoming the "package" in whatever form it arrives, knowing that your "Parent" knows best. If you continue to do so with trust and reverence, it should bring you a step closer to "living happily ever after." And, of course, that will be only the beginning of your story!

It sounds like a fairy tale! What's the catch? There isn't any, except that you must find it within you to sustain the process. Like anything new that you take up, the initial enthusiasm is the vehicle. It carries you for quite a distance, but then it wears off and you begin to "shirk" the practice. You find excuses not to do it. One "mess-up" and you're ready to believe it doesn't work. You lose momentum and sometimes go back to your old ways. This new way of living is the same—you need consistent practice, but the rewards are immeasurable.

When you go to a new yoga class, for example, you admire the instructor: Her body is flexible and beautiful, and she does all the asanas with ease. You want to emulate her. But you don't attempt to stand on your head and do everything she can in the first class. You work at it, slowly and gradually, stretching and pushing yourself. Eventually, your body opens up and becomes obedient. Every day, you bend a little farther, your arms get stronger, and your waistline shrinks. And when you're ready, you put your head on the ground, balance, and are doing a handstand!

It's the same with the practice of awareness, co-creation, and living life in a childlike manner. Keep at it. Strengthen the muscles. Become flexible. Stretch yourself. And soon—sooner than you think—it will all seem effortless.

The gift that you'll receive when you come to this point of flow is one that will thrill you . . . it's that of insight and intuition, which will now begin to guide and uplift you.

Chapter 15

THE BIGGER PICTURE

*"As a child of God, I am greater than
anything that can happen to me."*

— DR. A. P. J. ABDUL KALAM

*In*sight and *int*uition, as the words imply, flow from
within. They have the ability to show you the Bigger Picture. Sometimes, it may even look upside down, as if you
were really seeing it while standing on your head!

My everyday surroundings and seemingly ordinary
incidents appear to be rich with insights. I would like to
share three of them with you.

1. On one of my visits to a multistoried mall in the
city where I live, I was standing on the top floor, looking down at the various goings-on below me. I could see
so much in one glance: shoppers walking around—some

purposeful, others obviously browsing. I noticed a couple holding hands, oblivious to the hustle and bustle around them. A mother struggled with her baby's stroller. A man popped out of a shop to help her. Two people sat at a restaurant, obviously sulking in each other's company. An irate customer argued with the waiter at the coffee shop. I could hear her strident voice where I stood.

Here's an incident that caught my attention: I could see a young woman sitting at a table in the coffee shop. After a while, I noticed that she was getting agitated. She glanced at her watch every few minutes. It was apparent that she was waiting for someone who was late. As she continued to sit there, her restlessness increased. Evidently, her cell phone wasn't working or she'd forgotten to bring it along. Then, from that height, I suddenly saw a young man rushing over, also looking flustered. Perhaps he was the person she was waiting for. I could see from where I stood that he would reach her soon; he was on his way, but it would still take a few moments more. Meanwhile, her anxiety was mounting. She couldn't know from where she sat that he'd be with her shortly. He, too, had no way to assure her. From that "heightened perspective," though, I could see that all would soon be well.

Do you get the point I'm making? Stuck in our "ground-level views," we can only fret and fume and wonder when and how the situation will be resolved. We don't even know that there's a bigger picture, a different perspective. The insight struck me as I stood there: Of course there's a Bigger Picture. It's always in operation, and at no moment is any situation stationary.

When you see things from the ground level, what makes you feel hopeless and despairing is exactly this: the fact that you think things aren't moving and never will. But that's not the truth. From a higher perspective, you can see that indeed they're in the process of resolution in the most perfect manner possible. And there's so much more happening. In fact, each situation, to which you ascribe so much importance, is merely a dot—and pretty insignificant at that!

However, you can only look at things from where you are and what you've chosen to focus on! When you're caught in a troubling situation, if only you could change the "lens," you might be able to see a lot more than the limited area you're presently concentrating on. You might be able to see not just what's gone wrong, which is the thought presently consuming you, but also what *hasn't* and could have! In fact, you'd see that it's just a tiny part of a very big plan, which has its own purpose and rhythm. Change the lens from zoom to panoramic and see how it alters the picture you're looking at!

And how about applying this change to Life in general? Is there a Bigger Picture about you and *your* purpose, for example? Why are you here? What have you come to do?

I'm sure you've pondered these questions, too. Put the book down and think about them now. . . . What answer did you come up with? Did you identify your prime purpose as being a good wife, mother, or daughter? Father, son, or brother? How about being a teacher, a doctor, a lawyer, or whatever other type of professional you happen to be? Maybe you can identify your purpose with excelling at dance, music, painting, or filmmaking?

Actually, these are all roles that entail responsibilities: the "outer work." The real purpose of life—any life—is growth: soul growth . . . the "inner work." Unfortunately, the prioritizing of the two has gotten reversed. The "outer" has taken precedence over the "inner," which, in some cases, has been totally forgotten. That sounds bizarre, doesn't it, when you realize that it's the reason you've chosen to be incarnated on Earth?

> *"Thinking about sense-objects*
> *Will attach you to sense-objects;*
> *Grow attached, and you become addicted;*
> *Thwart your addiction, it turns to anger;*
> *Be angry, and you confuse your mind;*
> *Confuse your mind, you forget the lesson of experience;*
> *Forget experience, you lose discrimination;*
> *Lose discrimination, and you miss life's only purpose."*

— Bhagavad Gita

A lifetime on Earth is like a "training ground" to get an education, to enjoy, to repay debts, and to complete stories. Yes, to complete stories. Gary Zukav, a well-known author and self-empowerment guru, likens it to continuity in a television series that plays every week. Some of the central characters remain the same throughout. Others finish their roles and aren't seen in future episodes. They've "completed" what they had to do and say. Every week the story continues from where it left off in the previous one.

This is similar to how we live out our lifetimes, continuing the story, life after life, until it concludes. As we follow the main thread of the story, in each lifetime—as in each episode of the television series—the agenda and focus differ. After all, if every incarnation is a playground to experience and learn, there's much to be done. We have to experience fulfillment in many fields. We must enjoy fame, riches, physical pleasures, achievements, success in different activities, or the honing of a creative potential. When we've had our fill, we may choose to experience the opposite things—poverty, bankruptcy, violence, and abuse—for the "lessons" they offer. Debts certainly have to be repaid. Coming to terms with people and circumstances is also a consideration that's kept in mind.

> *"Here is a test to find whether your mission*
> *on earth is finished: If you're alive, it isn't."*

— from *Illusions,* by Richard Bach

There are certain emotions that we find hard to handle. We may choose to work on one or more of them in an "episode." Some of the obvious examples are anger, jealousy, guilt, insecurity, low self-esteem, hurt, and the like. In other lifetimes, we may choose to perfect "skills" like tolerance, forgiveness, acceptance, faith, surrender, joyfulness, gratitude, sacrifice, patience, flow, courage, responsibility, unconditional love, trust, and so on.

After a lifetime of "strenuous work," we may decide to take a break and just relax. We would then choose happy circumstances, harmonious relationships, and a comfortable life in which we can take a vacation before we get back to the grind. Each time around, we choose differently. Accordingly, we pick a role for ourselves, apart from the circumstances and players, in conjunction with the "syllabus" that we've set for that particular episode. This "syllabus" obviously includes elements that we may not have mastered or experienced as yet in other lifetimes.

For example, imagine that this time around, you've chosen to work on forgiveness. You'll set up your life circumstances accordingly. Obviously, you'll build in "tests" that will help you achieve your goal. Here are some possible scenarios: People could let you down, colleagues might betray you, and circumstances may work against you. And in each case you'll have a choice—learn the lesson, pass the test, or opt out. It's not random that each of us finds patterns being repeated in our lives. If you look closely, you might discover the same "lesson" hidden in each. Now obviously, once you've graduated after doing a particular course, you don't have to repeat it. You can next "register" for something else.

Our lives look different because each of us has chosen a unique mix of "courses." A mother working on giving unconditional love may be blessed with a disabled child to help her perfect it; a soul that has chosen patience may have to cope with a recurring illness or a life confined to a wheelchair; one wanting to give up anger and hone the skill of tolerance may be constantly needled, irritated, and provoked by a particular person in his or her life. Someone trying to give up control and learn surrender will face defiance; an individual seeking to master self-validation will be set up against a control freak. A row of adverse circumstances might have been selected to teach surrender and faith or, then, trust. It may be a lifetime of meager means chosen in order to learn humility and perfect the skill of receiving.

Can you see how elegant and benevolent the system is? Can you discern how intricately and delicately planned it is to help us achieve our goal at our own pace and rhythm? Can you also comprehend how irrelevant it is to moan about hard times, things not going according to "plan," people not treating us as we think we deserve to be, illnesses that befall us, businesses that falter and fail, relationships that crumble and disappoint, and circumstances that change the directions of our lives? Each serves as a small or big test that we need to pass to complete the particular "course" we've chosen.

"The world is a grand moral gymnasium
wherein we have all to take exercise so as
to become stronger and stronger spiritually."

— Swami Vivekananda

Look at your own life from this perspective. Appreciate the setup instead of complaining about it. It gives you a chance to learn. Become aware, too, that the lessons are "kindly" graded: They start at an elementary level and build up to that of "high school" and then graduation from college! If you're facing a particularly difficult test, you can congratulate yourself that you've progressed from the basic levels! Above all, be grateful to the faculty.

Who comprises this "faculty"? There are some people in your life who love, support, and understand you. There are others who help you or give you what you need. In turn, you do the same for them. There are those to whom you feel inexplicably bonded and many with whom you feel no connection, no matter how often you meet.

And then there are people with whom you're at loggerheads. They're the ones you rail and rant against the most. Prominent among them would certainly be someone close to you: a husband, a mother, a wife, a father, or a belligerent boss. This person is the one who has agreed to play the most relevant part in your "drama." He or she is someone who's spiritually very close to you, who loves you dearly even though the opposite seems to be the case in real life! That counterpoint, the "devil" in the play, the "thorn in your side," that wrecker of your happiness, is the person for whom you need to be the most thankful. This is the strict professor whom you might hate for the time being but for whom one day, when you really think about it, you'll have the most gratitude. Without him or her, it might be very difficult for you to learn your soul lesson, whatever it may be.

And it's the same with the circumstances you've faced. Very often you may have come up against hard times, marked by failure, defeat, rejection, insecurity, sickness, or loss. Many times, each setback might have changed the very direction of your life. Often you can look back on such hard times and see the good in them. If it's not so obvious, ask yourself what you gained from the difficult period.

If what remains is regret, resentment, hurt, bitterness, or envy, it means that you've lost sight of the lesson you were supposed to learn or have squandered the invisible opportunity for growth. If, however, this period fostered trust, faith, surrender, or flow, the pain it caused is a small price to pay! Hidden unobtrusively behind the everyday successes and—even likelier—the failures in our lives, are the more lasting achievements. Failing at a job, a relationship, or a business isn't as big a loss as it may seem at the time. Not being able to go beyond such a failure in order to learn the hidden "lesson" or understand its perfection for your growth is the real loss.

*"That's what learning is, after all . . . not whether
we lose the game, but how we lose and how we've
changed because of it and what we take away from
it that we never had before, to apply to other games.
Losing, in a curious way, is winning."*

— from *The Bridge Across Forever,* by Richard Bach

In other words, there is obviously a bigger plan than what you can see. Unlike what it may sometimes seem, it's a benevolent plan that you've sketched out for yourself. Having done that and set up the necessary "role-plays" to facilitate your plan, you still have a choice when you actually face the situation to bypass it or postpone it until another time. When, however, you can rise up to remember that it's only a "setup" and see the Bigger Picture, you'll find yourself grateful for, and accepting of, the manner in which your life unfolds.

Most important, you'll also begin to sense, and then live in the faith, that indeed there is a Higher Force—God, the Universe, a Divine Intelligence . . . you can choose the phrase that resonates with you the best—that's actually "running the show." And you can relax and allow it to! It does know best.

Remember, too, that the higher the level you can view your life from, the easier it will be to realize that you and your circumstances are just a small dot in the total scheme. Give yourself and your troubles a little less importance!

Close your eyes and think about your life (put the book down). How do you feel about it? Do you know what particular lessons you've come here to learn? Are the setup and the faculty not perfectly suited for the job? Does seeing this Bigger Picture make you feel differently about it?

I hope so.

*"I know God will not give me anything I can't handle.
I just wish that He didn't trust me so much."*

— Mother Teresa

2. Here is another insight I'd like to share.

I was waiting in the checkout line of a department store to pay my bill. When his turn came, the gentleman right in front of me made his payment and went over to the delivery desk to collect his package. Suddenly, everyone present heard a very distressed shout: "But how could you have done that? What did I do to deserve this?" His package had been mistakenly given to someone else. "But how could this have happened?" he repeatedly questioned. "What did I do to deserve this?" He was nearly hysterical.

And here's the thought that struck me: *Whenever something disturbing happens, these are the two questions we repeatedly ask.* The first one seeks to pin the blame on someone; the second aims to find a reason.

Sometimes there's no one to blame; it's no one's fault, yet things do go "wrong." And if they do, I want to know the reason! Somehow I feel that if someone explained to me why I deserved this, I would be able to "take" it. But if I'm a "good" person, who hasn't harmed anyone, and I feel that I don't deserve this fate, then I'm bewildered. I think Life is unfair. And that, as much as the circumstance, becomes the reason for my misery!

Neither question has an answer. The sooner you drop them, the more quickly you can begin to accept that it's just Life taking its course. The Universe doesn't believe in a system of punishments and rewards as you might think!

In fact, if anything, it's *all* a reward, a precious piece of that jigsaw puzzle called the Bigger Picture.

3. The third incident that transforms my perception every time I think of it happened on a recent flight. It was a rainy day. Gray clouds covered the horizon. Lightning occasionally streaked across the sky. Shortly, we took off. We were asked to keep our seat belts on because of the turbulent weather. In another half hour, I looked out. The sun sparkled brightly. The sky, a brilliant blue, stretched out all around us, vast and infinite.

This is how it always is, I thought. *Above the clouds, beyond the turbulence and the stormy weather, it's always clear and calm.*

No matter how ferocious the storm or how hard it rains—no matter how "permanent" this seems at the time—it's only a cloud, a passing phase. Although you may not be able to see it then, the sky is always there: blue, bright, unchanged.

In the midst of a troubled period, when it seems as if it will never pass, whisper to yourself: "It's only a cloud, not the sky."

> *"We are not unhappy today because of the complexities of life. We are unhappy because we miss its underlying simplicities."*
>
> — from *Life Lessons,* by Elisabeth Kübler-Ross and David Kessler

So use whichever of these everyday vignettes you resonate with. The next time you're upset, switch to the panoramic lens and drop the questioning. Remember that there's a Bigger Picture, even if you can't see it at that moment. If that doesn't work, look up at the sky; witness its vastness and know that your situation— a drifting cloud, already moving now—will pass.

❁ ❁ ❁

Chapter 16

INTEGRATION

*"An acorn makes no sense unless we
know that woven into the way it is made,
there is something waiting to unfold that
knows how to become an oak tree."*

— RACHEL NAOMI REMEN, M.D.

To be able to choose wiser perspectives, to access insight and intuition, and to listen to the voice of the Higher Self, we come full circle, back to where we started from. I posed a number of questions at the beginning of the book: How do you gauge the efficiency of your energy system and keep it in good shape? How do you prevent energy thieves from stealing your energy? Can you choose the states you wish to dwell in?

I hope this book has helped you shift some perceptions. The gauge for the "wellness" of your energy system is your e-motions. If you're feeling joyful, contented, grateful, alert, and expansive, your system is faring well. If you're not quite so comfortable, this will shine the light on resistance that you're up against or illuminate some energy thieves that are enjoying a "feast" at your expense. You know the solution: Plug the leaks—in other words, drop the resistance, face the fear, banish the worry, or exercise forgiveness, as the case may be.

Once you plug those leaks, your energy system immediately begins to recover. The disappearance of painful physical symptoms attests to the release of toxins! As you continue to "detoxify" yourself, your self-awareness increases. You begin to choose your responses and hence, shift the whole paradigm you're living in. You assume total responsibility for whatever state you find yourself in and know that only you, and not external circumstances, can resolve any problems that may crop up.

I discussed understanding the mind and Ego and being in charge. In actuality, this journey is about letting your mind, the small one that you're familiar with, dissolve and expand into the Big Mind, the place of infinite potential. Tapping into it allows you flow, surrender, co-creation, and higher guidance. The heart, remembered, guides you to increasing connectivity, joy, and love. It replaces pain as a habit.

This journey has to be *lived*, not merely understood.

Only the vibrancy and robustness of your energy system, the carrier of the vital force, will eventually help you to translate intellectual understanding into a way of being. Now, you may understand that worry does you no good; it drains you. Similarly, you're aware that hurt hurts. You know from experience that anger burns *you* up more than the person it's directed toward. You may sincerely wish to forgive, but you can't get yourself to do it.

You understand that you're responsible for your own state of happiness or unhappiness, but at some points you just can't *be* any happier! You don't feel like thinking positive or practicing any of the methods you've learned! You don't feel like attaining a state of flow; neither do you want to trust or surrender! You don't wish to be reminded that there's a Bigger Picture!

If only intellectual understanding could shift your state, you should be able to read one book on positive thinking or healing yourself or being happy and just follow the instructions therein! It doesn't work like that in real life, does it?

Many of us who are striving to live with awareness often feel frustrated because, although we understand and know what the right response could be, we still fall into habitual patterns, get tripped up by the Ego, or begin to leak energy to forbidden areas.

Well, don't leak more energy feeling guilty about such a situation. The truth is, at that particular moment, you don't have the necessary energy resources to do any better. Obviously, what I'm speaking about here isn't physical energy, strength, or stamina. I'm referring to a level of growth—a more accurate expression would be a "level of consciousness."

Each level allows you a greater degree of "translation." First, you understand what you have to do; perhaps you initially struggle with it and then suddenly, you find you can actually do it. For instance, you're drowning in a well of self-pity. Then one fine day, you find you can jump out of the well. You get hurt but realize that you can let go of it; you lose your cool but find that you can quickly get centered again. And, day by day, the time lag keeps shortening.

Intellectually understanding something is one part of the story. Actually beginning to *live* it is the other. I'm sure there are many methods of achieving this objective, but in my understanding, this "alchemy"—for it's nothing short of that—is possible only when this understanding is combined with a profound spiritual practice. Whether it's meditation, chanting, prayer, yoga, or any other technique, reverent and consistent practice is the only way. It's the internal cleansing I talked about that brings about the organic change. Such cleansing will help you operate at a consistently "higher" level, ensuring that you enjoy every moment of life's journey.

I would hesitate to prescribe any one method, because there's none that suits all. However, I would like to share those that have worked for me. During my journey, Reiki, the Art of Living techniques, and Emotional Freedom Techniques (EFT) have enriched me immeasurably. Since the scope of this book doesn't permit me to go into a detailed elucidation of each, anyone interested in them can find excellent books or resource material on the Internet. There are many sites that discuss Reiki, the gentlest and the most transformative energy that heals and makes whole. Details of the Art of Living Course, now taught in more than 150 countries, can be accessed at **artofliving.org**. And EFT (**emofree.com**) clears past and present distress, aches and pains, traumas, and fears in minutes! Recently I've been introduced to ThetaHealing, which also works miracles instantly.

Whichever practice you choose forms the "base" for your growth. Its value can't be underestimated.

In addition, you can start on your journey right now by doing some of the following:

— **Maintain a Gratitude Journal.** Every night, write ten things that you're grateful for in a journal kept especially for this purpose. Start each page with the sentence: "Today I am grateful for . . ." Every week increase the number of things by five or as many as you feel comfortable with. The ultimate aim is to build it up to 50, then 100, and even more.

Perhaps you think this is some fake, feel-good exercise. It's not. It's one of the most profoundly transformative yet simple processes you could follow.

Here's what the process does: It gets you to focus on what's good in your life, not on what isn't. And it's a proven energy rule: *What you focus on expands.* This is the easiest way of attracting more of what makes you happy.

And it's the easiest way of being open to receive. Do you know that very often the Universe is ready to manifest your desires, but finds the door locked when it knocks to deliver them? Gratitude, quite simply, raises your vibrations to receive what you wish for.

Additionally, can you imagine what would happen when you're writing 100 or more things in your list every day? You'd have moved from the five to ten "essentials"—your physical surroundings, family, food, health, and so on—to really being alive virtually every moment. When your list is really long—and growing—you'll be noticing and feeling grateful for the sunset, the smile of a beggar, the cup of tea someone made for you, the cat curled up against your leg, the fragrance of jasmine in the night breeze, the taste of mango, the . . . Can you begin to see how aware and present you would be?

The Gratitude Journal moves you from an Ego space to a Higher Self space, from the zoom to the panoramic lens.

— **Meditate.** I mentioned this activity in an earlier chapter. Meditation provides the break that your mind needs and deserves. This is a basic requirement—not a luxury or choice—necessary to cope with today's highly stressed lifestyles.

Again, if you're one of those who can't understand the power of meditation, this scientific explanation might make sense. When you're in action mode, the mind is in a beta state. It's alert and focused. If the pattern of brain waves is measured, it would range between 14 Hz (hertz) and about 100 Hz. The higher range would indicate a level of restlessness or fear.

A more relaxed brain would be in the alpha, semi-awake state you're in just before you fall asleep or wake up fully. The brain-wave activity would be in the range of 8 Hz to 14 Hz. This is the time for making intentions, and it's quite effective because the conscious mind is largely absent and unable to obstruct you!

A still more relaxed mode is the theta state, in which the brain waves would be between 4 Hz and 8 Hz. This is usually the state when we're sleeping and may be dreaming. ThetaHealing is a particular modality that helps the practitioner reach it yet be "awake" to facilitate deep and instant healing. It's probably the state in which many creative geniuses, inventors, and scientists experienced their "Eureka!" moments.

A still deeper level of consciousness is the delta state, in which the brain-wave activity dips to below 4 Hz, when we're in deep sleep and probably not dreaming.

When you meditate, the brain-wave activity actually slows down, and depending on the depth of your meditation, you can access more profound levels of creativity, healing, relaxation, and de-stressing. This is the time when the small mind actually plugs into the Big Mind, gets recharged, and accesses an area of infinite potentiality.

There could be nothing simpler than sitting and letting go and just *being* to produce such amazing results.

If you feel unsure about how to begin or what to do, seek out a teacher who can guide you and offer some structure to help you get started, or else you can join a formal class and use it as long as you need it.

— **Breathe!** Make a small placard that displays this one word. Put it on your office desk or at home where you can see it frequently. Every time you do, just take *two* deep breaths with awareness and continue with your regular activities. Alternatively, let your cell phone or alarm clock remind you to do this every hour or as often as is comfortable. This is an incredible awareness exercise. It helps you create the space you need to make conscious choices.

— **Cut cords.** This is a magical practice. When we interact with people, we're automatically connected to them by a cord at the solar plexus (the area just below the rib cage). We "exchange" energies through this cord— which is strong in the case of people we're close to.

To keep your energy system clear, you must disconnect and terminate this exchange each day with every person you interact with. It's an excellent practice if you've had an unpleasant conversation with someone. You can even try it in the middle of an argument and will see dramatic results. You must do it at least once, at the end of the day—and more often if you feel you particularly need it with some people.

This is what you do: Close your eyes. Visualize the cord. Imagine yourself cutting it. Mentally say: *I cut and release all connections with you at the solar-plexus level.* Reconnect the cord at the heart level. Say the words: *Only love remains between us.*

This wonderful little technique brings harmony into relationships, raises them to a totally different level, keeps your energy system clear, and prevents energy drains. It's an essential daily "cleanser."

— **Steal joy.** This is an amazing practice that you can use to "trick" yourself into changing your mood or state when you're feeling miserable, let down, or anxious. First of all, accept that this is so and allow it to be. Don't fight it. But offer yourself a break from your misery, for just a day. Have a conversation with yourself that goes something like this: "I know you're miserable, and I can understand that, but why don't you just take a day's break from worrying, hurting, being in fear, and so on? Just drop the issue for a day, steal some joy, even though it's not warranted at the moment, and you can go right back to being miserable tomorrow!"

If the miserable part of yourself (and it *is* only a part of you!) agrees, that's great news. Then go ahead and just be joyful, "normal," and happy for the day. And make yourself the same offer the next! However, there's a good chance that it will feel "irresponsible" to take so much time off, so then negotiate for a half day, a few hours, an hour, or even 15 minutes! Sounds funny? It's not. It's an excellent way of demonstrating to yourself that you're in charge of choosing your state . . . of realizing that you needn't remain a victim of circumstances. As you begin to understand and practice this, it becomes a way of living, and you no longer allow yourself to wallow in states that are draining and unhealthy for you.

Similarly, remind yourself, in whatever manner you choose, about the practices mentioned at different places in the book ("in the fire"; the Bigger Picture, or panoramic lens; and so forth).

Remember to constantly dissect your actions by rephrasing the question *Why is this happening to me?* as *Why is this happening?* It will immediately show you where you're placing your attention.

Injecting these little exercises in awareness into your daily life will make you feel in charge, starting immediately. They're indeed profound ways to shift your state almost instantly and take responsibility for yourself.

Chapter 17

FREE IN THE FOREST

*"The aim of life is to live, and to
live means to be aware, joyously,
drunkenly, serenely, divinely aware."*

— HENRY MILLER

As a teenager, my daughter painted a poignant canvas, one of 20 for an exhibition entitled *Freedom*. This one had a man clutching on to the bars of a prison cell. Upon closer observation, you could see a green forest right behind him. I questioned her about this. Yes, she explained, that's how she saw Life: Our fears, Ego, conditioning, mind-sets, worries, hurts, and doubts keep us imprisoned. If we could only let go of those bars and turn around, we would realize that, in fact, we're already free. The cell is an illusion. Right behind is a forest. The choice is with each of us whether we want to remain in that cell, clutching on to the bars, or walk free in the forest.

Are you ready to make that choice? Do you want . . .

. . . to continue to live in darkness or in the light of joyous awareness?

. . . to be in a state of resistance or in a state of flow?

. . . to remain a victim or be empowered?

. . . to fear Life or be in unconditional love with it?

Would you like to view Life standing on your head and see how things look upside down?
You might see . . .

. . . that real strength is personified by the gentleness of love, not domination through fear.

. . . that the power you have inside you is infinite compared with what you seek outside.

. . . that the Invisible Force that makes things happen is more real than any visible action.

. . . that flow is so much more relaxing than resistance and control.

. . . that you're responsible only for giving intent, and receiving abundance is your right.

. . . that Joy and Love are what you've come here to experience, preferably in every moment!

Are you ready for this magical journey?
Come on, fetus, curled up in your comfort zone, take a deep breath . . . and push yourself out into the light!

Acknowledgments

Many people have had a hand in "shaping" this book.

My husband, Ashok, first suggested I write it. He guided me to do it. He helped me to finish it after months of procrastination by setting a deadline I dared not disrespect!

V. K. Karthika, publisher and chief editor, Harper-Collins India, New Delhi, was the next "shaper." She listened indulgently when I described it as an adventure and explained that I was not sure exactly how it would look at the end. She let me write and express myself freely, and then with an experienced editor's keen eye, guided me firmly and ruthlessly to giving the book its present form. I owe her a debt of gratitude I will never be able to fully express.

Ashok Malik first edited the manuscript with sensitivity and competence. K. J. Ravinder put the final touches to it, going through it with a meticulously keen eye for detail and an amazing thoroughness without, in any way, detracting from the essence or content.

Many teachers shaped my ideas and taught me, through their writings, techniques, and courses I chose to do. My earliest teachers, for whom I have the deepest admiration and respect, are Louise Hay, Shakti Gawain, Caroline Myss, and Gary Zukav. They are as "real" to me as others who later taught me some of the therapies that have become a way of life for me. Puran and Suman initiated me into Reiki, a divine energy that remains a powerful guiding force for me. From Holly Holmes Meredith, I have received love, wisdom, and one of the most magical tools I practice: Emotional Freedom Techniques. Working with this tool, seeing people being healed in minutes, and watching patterns shift before my eyes have never ceased to amaze me. From Sunny Satin, under the guise of hypnotherapy, I learned something much more meaningful: secrets of the soul, the perfection of a Universal Plan, and the infinity of past and future lives. And from Tathagat, the art of living fully in the present one. One teacher I remember especially fondly, even though I met her only twice, has been Sally Perry. She worked in mysterious ways, and I am sure I do not still fully understand how much she did for me.

My father-in-law (Balraj Chopra) shared many nuggets of wisdom about his understanding of life and living.

Neel Advani always kept me generously supplied with information, knowledge, and books reflecting new paradigms in my areas of interest. Though an aunt by relationship, she has in the last few years become more of a dear friend and fellow traveler on this journey of growth.

Agnese (Barolo Rizvi), Arti (Khosla), Tammi (Brughuis), and Gargi (Sen), my wise clairvoyant friends, gave me, at different times of my life, the gifts of a richer, deeper understanding. Effortlessly, magically, matter-of-factly, they made the invisible, visible; the hidden, obvious. Though I didn't realize it at the time, each of them subtly "turned" the direction of my life.

Harish Nirula and Kaywan continue to teach me by example. He epitomizes quiet wisdom and unconditional love; she demonstrates living every moment with awareness disguised as bubbly verve.

Taarini, my fearless, focused, compassionately detached daughter talked, painted, and discussed with me the invisible bedrock of this book and her credo in life: the concept of freedom. I feel sure that she and Ashok are the special faculty selected to help me learn the lessons I have chosen for this lifetime.

My dearest friends, Usha (Chengappa) and Aneeta (Bansal), have lovingly held my hand along this incredible adventure. Through our endless discussions and honest sharing of each other's lives, we have "cracked many mysteries," excavated hidden subtleties and profundities from most situations, and, above all, delighted in the "parallel-ness" of our journeys. Antonella (Mathur), a fellow traveler and dispenser of magical potions, envelops me in love, understanding, and a profoundly gentle wisdom every time we meet.

I will perhaps never be able to adequately acknowledge each one of my "students," who honored me by coming to my workshops, follow-up sessions, and discussion groups. Over the years, their questions challenged me, their expectations inspired me, and their openness and sharing taught me humility. Many of them taught me patience! Their faith, love, and confidence have made me the "teacher" I am today.

No matter what I have chosen to do, my parents (Kamla and R. P. Singh) have offered me love and understanding, as have my guides.

I feel blessed.

— R.S.

✺ ✺ ✺

About the Author

Rohini Singh has written eight best-selling cook-books and two novels for children. She practices a number of alternative healing therapies, including Reiki, reflexology, hypnotherapy, Emotional Freedom Techniques, and ThetaHealing; and conducts regular personal-growth workshops and healing retreats both in India and elsewhere.

We hope you enjoyed this Hay House book. If you'd like to receive a free catalog featuring additional Hay House books and products, or if you'd like information about the Hay Foundation, please contact:

Hay House, Inc.
P.O. Box 5100
Carlsbad, CA 92018-5100

(760) 431-7695 or **(800) 654-5126**
(760) 431-6948 (fax) or **(800) 650-5115 (fax)**
www.hayhouse.com® • **www.hayfoundation.org**

Published and distributed in Australia by: Hay House Australia Pty. Ltd., 18/36 Ralph St., Alexandria NSW 2015 • *Phone:* 612-9669-4299 *Fax:* 612-9669-4144 • www.hayhouse.com.au

Published and distributed in the United Kingdom by: Hay House UK, Ltd., 292B Kensal Rd., London W10 5BE • *Phone:* 44-20-8962-1230 • *Fax:* 44-20-8962-1239 • www.hayhouse.co.uk

Published and distributed in the Republic of South Africa by: Hay House SA (Pty), Ltd., P.O. Box 990, Witkoppen 2068 • *Phone/Fax:* 27-11-467-8904 • orders@psdprom.co.za • www.hayhouse.co.za

Published in India by: Hay House Publishers India, Muskaan Complex, Plot No. 3, B-2, Vasant Kunj, New Delhi 110 070 • *Phone:* 91-11-4176-1620 • *Fax:* 91-11-4176-1630 • www.hayhouse.co.in

Distributed in Canada by: Raincoast, 9050 Shaughnessy St., Vancouver, B.C. V6P 6E5 • *Phone:* (604) 323-7100 *Fax:* (604) 323-2600 • www.raincoast.com

Tune in to **HayHouseRadio.com®** for the best in inspirational talk radio featuring top Hay House authors! And, sign up via the Hay House USA Website to receive the Hay House online newsletter and stay informed about what's going on with your favorite authors. You'll receive bimonthly announcements about Discounts and Offers, Special Events, Product Highlights, Free Excerpts, Giveaways, and more!
www.hayhouse.com®